**Lakeland**

Maureen O'Shaughnessy

# Lakeland

## Acknowledgements

For their support and assistance special thanks are due to my mother, my cousin Almut, and Hardwig and Siegfried. Thanks also to my father, whose commitment to poetry was inspirational; to Debra Adelaide who, as an early reader of a part of this book, helped with important feedback; to Sue Hurley for her guidance as a later reader; to takt kunstraumprojektum for providing a three-month residency in Berlin; and to Helen Garner. And for their endless patience, ideas and encouragement, without which this book would not have been possible, I wish to give particular thanks to my daughter Claude and husband Martin.

For Leni

*Lakeland*
ISBN 978 1 76041 044 5
Copyright © text Maureen O'Shaughnessy 2015

First published 2015 by
**GINNINDERRA PRESS**
PO Box 3461 Port Adelaide 5015
www.ginninderrapress.com.au

# Contents

| | |
|---|---|
| Arrival | 9 |
| Fragmentblatt (Leaf Fragments) | 11 |
| In the Wind's Way | 31 |
| Wasserturm (Water Tower) | 45 |
| Dear Sister | 57 |
| The Masurian Lakes | 61 |
| Second Language | 83 |
| What Name Will You See When You Do Not Hear a Sound? | 95 |
| Rope in the Snow | 99 |
| Kabinet of Pink Bits | 119 |
| Epic Angels | 137 |
| October in the Northern Hemisphere | 143 |

Stand too close to horror, and you get fixation, paralysis, engulfment; stand too far, and you get voyeurism or forgetting. Distance matters.

Eva Hoffman, *After Such Knowledge*

# Arrival

## Sieglinde
## Sydney Harbour, April 1963

> A light from forests breaks through the ruby dust.
> Enchanted an opera house shines in the grey.
> — Trakl

Once bent winds chiselled the water in bluish spirals
quiet as gloves.
She thought, now I'm going to be held
forever.
And the wind stayed with them, blazing on the deck
and blazing, and it didn't go away.

# Fragmentblatt (Leaf Fragments)

## M
### Melbourne, 1989

> And the dear, round lamp-
> moon appears in the house...
> How small life is here
> and how big nothingness.
> — Robert Walser

**i**

It was the fifth morning and I heard her all night,
a woman — I ought to say my mother — in her room.

Calls (3 a.m.) from hospital.
That radio beating on,

beating on, cellos against horns. And calls, (5 a.m.)
more calls (6 a.m.) — and I ask myself
who is it now? and the radio

beating on.

Disquiet inside me, like a girl on a first date.

Melbourne — a deputy premier
the *Herald-Sun* calls Mother Russia,

and cricket from Lord's on a borrowed television,

and my father, who left this world astonishingly often,

was coming and going continuously,
like someone opening a door and looking through
and shutting it and opening and looking through.

Daybreak: I took their dog for walks.
It was a time of practical matters – and waiting.

**ii**

Always on these visits – it's what
you take in. A strip of window
framing blue sky over the casuarinas. The sound of
the dryer. A cluttered living room.
Gleam

on veneer drawers and
eels of light.
Cicadas' song
in the sun of near-end February.
Standing there, musing

on the form of houses,
the effects of lighting
on the arrangement of things,
marks of habit in brick
and strips of exposed wood:

and on your mother down the hall,
fatigue under her eyes,
working to maintain
a level world;
finding force in never hesitating,

never pausing, the sole way
of her knowing
is in her going on with life,
and her going on.
There.

### iii

'When she was pregnant,' my sister said,
'she says he went to the bank manager
for a loan for a nightie.'

### iv

Improbable
radius of the words, lines
of love that were the streams to the basin

then fog hovering, over
the wide calm of the lake.

A sleight of the mind's eye,
like a bed without sheets.

### v

I make you a picture of her as I saw it.
Moulded twists of grey hair pinned as from childhood.
And the fluent crepe dressing gown falling over curves
of the fullest contour, blue with a gold border,
finest piping of gold snaking along the collar
like a *Lindwurm* wending all the way up to her neck.
Down the stairs, slapping in felt slippers
with hands in her pockets, glancing out of the window
at the same concrete patio, the same unsettled trees,

the same grey fence line and the same tiled roofs she'd been
looking at for such a long time. Anxiety was it.
The alarm of a hot February north wind picking up.
And waft after waft of vacancy.
No children in the house any more.

Shadows feeding on the petal-strewn grass.
Crab apples and elders and banksias scattering
drying leaves on the double-brick homes
spread across the reclaimed billabong.
Antennae cables swinging in the cloudless breeze.
And the clip and ting of a dripping tap,
the implacable drawl of a distant freeway,
the soddening of onions in a wicker basket,
the stink of the vinegar in which she had cooked
for dinner last night the pot of red cabbage.

### vi

The problem was, trying to arrive at strength
when the days are open mystery; *stabil* or stable,
I discover when looking it up, having come from the old French word
*estable* for 'standing room'. It was an impossible measure
between two points. You are never
not questioning when it might happen, trying
to pick up on the signals,
like an old card player. You are never not there

and also somewhere else.
Stable is the space between the wall and the door.

### vii

From her angle, a gap bridging
the two conditions of myth or nothing.
That morning, her face floating in the mirror.

He's in a ward: him and her,
they are gratified by the long days
of togetherness apart. Separate togetherness.

That morning, her face floating in the mirror.
Still his heart tugging without limit
on life in its usual way – the simple

determined action of the body
circulated by blood flowing
round bone and muscle,
the intricate equipment that bears
what makes a human being,

bears existence,
the regarding self that asks
what is ending?

This was the other problem: I was sleeping in my old bedroom. I was twenty-six. I'd come down a week earlier after five years in Sydney, and the house was half shut up. I'd had no proper job for six months and had started smoking again, even though I had virtually no money and couldn't afford cigarettes. And my heart was overcome. In the mornings I often thought I was going to throw up. I was heading full tilt for divorce. The end was boundless.

**viii**

Perhaps as she said, it all came down to *Dialekte*.

In the street outside the hospital the night before, I'd noticed her slip in
half-eaten sandwiches, sachets of sugar, a little china milk jug,
taken from his tray,
then zip her bag.

My father was weak; he always had something
he couldn't finish eating, items my mother was expected
to store or hoard. But whatever conflicts
there may have been between them this wasn't one.

The anxiety of waste –

in the cupboards packets of cornflour, prunes,
crackers, long past their use-by date, displaced recollections
and granular archaic dust, and the vast crawling

intimacies of time.

Also, the nearness of separation.
But what if we were to speak of the fictions
of places? How families have their languages?
My mother's voice, her terrifying accent!

I still use the nicked Qantas knives on visits.
They were not for general distribution as she seems to have thought.

**ix**

All this happened years ago. But then – have you noticed? – how in your peripheral vision

> the horizon
> rises,
> and how
> you're propelled
> towards
> what previously
> existed,
> the weeks,
> hours, minutes
> piled up
> underneath
> to scale
> the line of vision.

First the desire, then the struggle, and then the image.

## x

You know how Werther watching Lotte cut bread for all those young siblings
sat entranced
at her domestic devotion
to the little children
tumbling with grotty hands and faces
and smiling abandon (and with smiling abandon buried himself)
perhaps this is what my father was thinking?
A vision. Of the future.
He liked Germans. Women
in blouses, sandals, woollen tights.
My mother
a dazzling au pair of twenty-one
when they met in Munich – he wore her obedience
like a wristwatch.
He was glad she didn't mind moving.
And then children, in breathless waves, turning up,
seven of them
in ten years, crowding
into the fifties bungalow one after the other, as promised:
on their first date, a Bruckner symphony,
> *as many offspring as this piece –*

he'd laughed.
Some prayers are answered.

From the table in the dining room I see my mother in the kitchen. She's stooped, though still tall, and she has dark blotches under her arms, and pale eyelids. She's cleaving the heel of a week-old rye loaf at the counter. I'm sitting at the far end of the table with a coffee in front of me. After a couple of minutes, she sits down opposite with two slices of toast, you could say doorstops, and some jam. I wonder what she might be thinking about. Yesterday, while having dinner, I heard her explain to my sister on the phone that she had put her faith in Our Lord. Then I happened to pick up the words 'fortnight', 'apple pie', 'eightieth birthday', 'of different values', 'the Pancake Parlour', 'sputum', 'whatever God wills'. When she'd hung up I didn't question her on the conversation. I wanted to know more about how she felt things ought to be, but I understood enough to know there was no point drawing her into something that she'd assume was confrontational. (Whatever God wills for him? For her? Whatever God wills for himself, et cetera?) God was, at the very least untroubled, or indifferent. Watching her now, at the table, spreading butter with small, precise gestures, I can see she sits calmly, but is uncomfortable, and I think maybe I didn't register the arrangement of her words as useful phrases because she seemed mysterious in some strange, vital way, and because of the chasm between us. The noise of a lawnmower starts up in the yard next door, drowning out the sound of her rhythmic chewing. When she's finished, she raises her head from her plate and says she doesn't think she'll make it into the hospital till late afternoon now, when my sisters will be there, and my oldest brother, and the thirty-two-year-old specialist who wants to share the latest test results before leaving for his holiday in Laos.

## xi

Lightness. I remember it, the effervescent surge.
At some point I began to fear the worst and I breathed myself into air;
it was like treading the surface of a dam.

'D'you want to go for a walk?' I used to shout to my brother
from the stairs, and he would always yell, 'Yes!'
from his bedroom, 'Yes!' and my mother would say,

'Not the little ones,' and, of course,
that's what suited us. That was what she was meant to say.
Mothers in the seventies couldn't track

though most days she had the soul of a sentinel,
and the eye and hand of a sentinel. If she'd said,
'Take the others with you,' then neither of us would have known

what to laugh about, which streets to pick, where we should head.
We laughed, tears streaming from our eyes, my brother and I,
stumbling in rapt circles along the footpath,

about the whole catastrophe of foreignness.
The implausible English, the ordered motion of her shrewd energies,
the foot-high fur hat she wore to church.

And where we went there was a creek –
bluish mists moving in winter in front of the new
hillside estate, the waterline edged

with reeds and slippery thick sludge, and the suck
suck suck of dawdling horses' hooves –
where we'd scull in the water filled with dark and tadpoles,

sieving handfuls of broken stones and sand, and tiny fish
snared from their shallows, the animate universe
of millennia ago. Looking back,

I see now what I thought of as a tug
between the restraint of home
and the hunger of long awaited departure

more as a continuous circling drive, rolling, incessant,
as if we were pitched against the pull of Charybdis' maw.
What we discovered in forms that pass between two worlds

is eternal movement, the drift and jerk of gravity on sinew
and heart, all nerve and design finding its way, in constant flux,
leaving traces of random loss, as well as progress –

evolution coming at you in spirals. Absence
was a game for us. Disappear if you think you want to.
Disappear if you can.


The wind raised the house; long mornings taking me through the light
years. Sitting at the table in the summer glare of the childhood living room,
I imagine my husband like this: he is alone, his clothes grubby, his eyes
hard, his face immaculate. He's stretching his arms into a leather jacket.
And then he's opening the door, trying to pull it shut behind him with one
foot, an unnecessary habit because the lock is the kind that has to be turned

or it's not secure anyway. The shutters are still drawn. Maybe he hasn't put the cover on his Ducati. On the side of the porch that collects dust and dead leaves, I can see the shadows the telegraph poles are throwing on the peeled walls and the concrete paving. I can see him from a distance, then close up. It's as if no time has passed, he looks like he did when I first met him. He is not just a beautiful man, he encompasses something else, according to the picture in my head anyway. He isn't tall, but his body, except for its slight lack of height, is perfectly proportioned, and gives the impression of being vigorous, even strapping, like the body of an athlete nearing peak form. All the same his strength seems psychological more than physical somehow. It's strange. Why am I conjuring up all this? I think I'm replaying a scene I'm not used to not seeing yet, that it's the scene that will help me in getting closer to the truth of things.

### xii

I was trying to rely on myself.
I wrote in an exercise book,
*There are all kinds of solitude.*

The wind was blustery and heat flooded the house.
If my mother was crying, in other words, I couldn't hear her.

That is what I remember: strained,
but all the sounds were blindly mechanical.

I wrote under the first line,
*The room is calm and silent…*

Lied to myself. And then made up stories
for the things I could no longer quite remember,

to make the versions manageable, to seal not salt the wounds.

*Can I become*
    *Can I become*
        *Can I become*

*someone else?*

Not here.

My brain in that place had a splinter in its finger.

We'd been together five years. We met in '83. I was kind of one of his friend's girlfriends. We were at a party, then as things started winding down I went home with him. He drove this red, noisy, outrageous ute, and told me about going to a private boys' school in Sydney's eastern suburbs after life in the far west of the state. When he'd first arrived, long hair was forbidden at school, but after he and some classmates wrote a series of formal protests, they changed the rule. Between that night and the next weekend we moved in together, and I was happy, and it was pretty good, and he was cheery, always kind of dancing with energy. Surprised at something or other.

## xiii

*How much do we get out of knowing certain people?*

How do you know these things?

He went on contemplating, moving his fingers and making smooth fragments of geometry across the small of my back and the elastic of my pants and the splotch of moles on my leg like broken eggshells.

With an expanse of confidence I wasn't used to, it wasn't long before his family were spending as much time with us as we'd allow them. What they liked more than anything were the holidays that we – his parents, sister, brother-in-law, and their kids – would take in rented beach houses. Family life to them was noticeably different from the ordinary systems that can kill. They mixed cocktails each night, and made lewd jokes and bravely ran their pleasures into one another. They helped install the second-hand kitchen in our sublet flat in Bondi Junction. This was during the time that he and I were doing a lot of mandies and coke. We were on a kind of treadmill of sex and obliteration. But if they came round, they crooned Wayne Newton songs, sat pleasantly having a drink with us, never saying a word.

**xiv**

Once he said, 'My father taught me how to love Banjo, boxing and my country.' His country? So many of his sentences began with a possessive pronoun.

Smack went my heart. I guess I was jealous.

Jealous. Is this really the word?

I guess I exaggerate.

But in trying to understand, you tell yourself there are countless different cities and faces, seeing things for the last time, but you never know that, or accept it perhaps, at that moment. You think maybe you couldn't take it in, that dream behind the eye, because of all those sleepless nights. You write, each tendon straining as if cramp had taken over your hand, while your mother marches into the room all of a sudden and gives you ten minutes to get dressed. When the time comes to leave, you decide to stay where you are anyway. You help her put her bags in the car and then go shut yourself up in the house, with a feeling like incredulity, because there is something universally mysterious about places where everything is unquestioned, assured.

**xv**

I thought that when someone loves you,
you are held from certain kinds of despair.

When I was very young, my father on weekends took me on his hospital rounds. We drove to the city in his new blue Rover. From the car I'd smell of leather, even hours later. I'd follow him through the wards, gaze at his bended back and want to sing with cheerfulness. Swift bright hum of relief; it cascaded through my body like the thaw of a mountain stream. I'd feel safer then than at any time in the heavy furnished rooms of the familial home. That was the hope I lived in: that we could hide from the rest of them out in the streets of East Melbourne. I felt I held him then.

Even the way he responded more readily to me than the appeals of 'Dr –.' He trusted me with my pink flowery dirndl high over my knees as I passed by the patients' faces and avoided their eyes. And then, on the days he went into his surgery, the feeling that mercy was elsewhere. Daydreams of his rooms. The women arriving. Hanging up their coats and lying on the white medical bed, with glances that say duty, decency, moving between them in silence, even as through the waves of pain and sickness and under the clattering chrome-edged light they're feeling the relief of impersonal tenderness, faded teal walls, and the thin glow of the bar heater, soaped skin, darkened windows, the calm of a watchful quiet there.

**xvi**

My husband was a sunny man. He could
have been thinking 'heal from what?' But I don't know.
His language had different names for things.

One day we were riding the bike along the lakes of Centennial Park together. He said, 'A thousand-cc motor, but you can do it.' He was on the back teaching me the controls. 'Clutch down for first, then up, then up, then up.' It was a blue afternoon, sheer as gin, the kind that spreads over the city with a degree of carelessness. To my right and to my left were rows of Moreton Bay figs. Mounting the crest of a hill, I screwed my fingers round the handles and squeezed hard. A split second between travelling at full speed and braking I realised it would be a tree I was hitting and dropped the bike. Later, almost imperceptibly, details will surface; the rubble-lined asphalt, the string of roots, the disintegrating Mars wrapper, the rolling cigarette lighter, the drag as a palm braces in the gravel breaking the impact that is made by velocity and the weight of a human being. But for that instant the whole thing was acted out like night falling in wide spilling blank sunlight and with casual fear, everything dissolving, as if we were at risk of turning invisible. I heard my husband's hand snap, and the flesh of my arm unzipped from wrist to elbow. Head on one side, sprawled on the ground in front of me, he flicked the little squares of Perspex with a finger of his good hand. 'They look like diamonds in the dirt there.'

## xvii

*My two youngest sisters are changing their babies' nappies on the sofa together.*

By the way, I won't come back tonight after all.
OK, tomorrow?
She can always ring if she's desperate.
What's the verdict then?
Can't tell.
You're the nurse.
I don't know – a week?
Crazy, isn't it.
Which bit?
Having no one but us.
Must be how they want it.
But on the verge of death, him reading his old poets, her just sitting there.
I stickied through some of his drawers yesterday.
Oh?
So much junk, including a letter – from 1936 – signed by Franco himself.
Huh. And he worries we've cost him eternal life.
How old was he then?
Sixteen, I guess. Pass me the wipes?
Must have been brainwashed.
In those days Catholic schools were full of priests who were fascist sympathisers.
Really?
The Irish loyalty thing.
Right: and there's one from a Dominican monk, about joining up.
Yeah, him in the army!
No, the priesthood – the monk says it wouldn't be right yet, too young.
Wow…you know he wouldn't have even got married if she hadn't converted.
Yes.
And you've heard he's made her promise never to remarry.
What?
Or sell the house, the old 'the mortar in those bricks is my blood' schtick.
Really?
Did she say it was OK to look at those letters?
She wasn't here.

Oh.
I folded them back with the rest of the papers, photos, tickets, cufflinks…
God, there's a lot of stuff in this place.
I've kept one thing, though, a Chekhov quote he's copied out.
Why? What about?
About medicine being his wife and writing his mistress, something like that.
Huh.
Don't make me feel guilty.
OK.
I'll put it back.
What?
The note.
I don't care.
Anyway, it looks like he's going to make the big eight-oh after all.
Yes, it would be bad for her if he died on the actual day, though.
Like her mother did, on your birthday M –…
*(me)* Yes.
Yes.
Yes.
Do you want me to microwave some mash for them?

*They pick up their babies and, cradling them gently in their arms, walk off towards the kitchen.*


## xviii

Watering vegetable beds in the garden
you're looking at where the earth, darkening,
sops up the spray, wormy clods balled in unweeded runnels, streaked
scattered stones spilling against wood and sand,
when deep by the roots you glimpse dots of decay –
grubs, rot, and think how behind any façade
lie the small betrayals: those brownish-purple lines
on your father's poled legs, for instance, his winter hands,
faint crystalline ridges streaking his chest
like an oar on the lake's surface, the thin wing of his collarbone.

What you think of is how, years before,
the pain was unbearable.
How it made you full and empty at once. How, when you left
there was a kind of uncurling that was all subtext:
the fantasy was that in leaving
there wouldn't be those unholy resentments any more
flowing and flowing, hidden... In Carlton, in a terrace house,
in a summery room, there was a man so easy in his beauty
that when you held his head, or turned your back
as he pressed his cock against you, or breathed
the liquid creviced air of where his thighs met,
some form of revelation never experienced made
a kind of comfort possible. Under the mirrors and the curtains
blurring like birds in the drifts of sky in front of the open window
and the plaintive-sounding tunes of Tim Buckley on the record player.
Pillocked dust round the lamp. Dust too, marbling the ledges
and that coat you used for a blanket. And that columny tinging that went on
and on from the leak in the rusted spouting... You'd been at a meeting
of the university Socialist Club that morning. South Africa
and nuclear disarmament. You were going through a stage
where you wanted all attachments incompatible with theirs.
The exposed heart of the Yellow Peril in the city square.
Or the Industrial Action campaign. This man
was part of that. You lay on the bed, your head
as high as a flock of birds and felt such blows of desire, and calm,
always attended by the declarations taking into consideration
fear, sex, the longing to please, et cetera –
there was no mystery in the sweetness of his being Jewish.
Also wine, drugs, the cigarettes, a bad haircut. Held together by bits
that were the opposite of everything – you knew it wasn't original.
Ultimately, the move on. (The junk and so forth.) No one sees
you unwind the road north; you never say goodbye to anyone either.
You drive away in a single night and have the sensation
of life just arriving. Meet others. Make vows. And don't look back
      for a long time.

So there's a certain language in coming back.
It carries in it the tenderness of what exists, the nerved surfacing
of what's resurrected, and the shape of space. Which may be why
there are always gaps in the experience of families.
Here, words are scattered like stepping-stones.
They weave among the blossoming spread of undergrowth, step
following step following step to the mythical scrub. When you walk,
you think mostly of what lives in between, works its way up.
And when you look to where the yard meets the sky,
you see snaky tendrils writing something on the dry air,
and boughs, wreathed with vines, like that sacred grove at Nemi, bent
along where the crab apple, flowering, froths up globs of vivid red.
The voices coming from the house make themselves familiar, the wind
winding the sound of them around the heaped branches.
And you hear your brother singing,
Fine Young Cannibals again, which is in tune (if you're lucky)
and the scarab beetles are whizzing in the fading light –
the idiosyncratic frantic motion, the wild bombing of the insect
happily targeting its mate – and for a moment, you can see
that there are all forms of there, and nothingness, in separation,
and even now, with your shoes sunk in the dirt,
how a story circles, fills to inhabit others.

So, suppose I went back to him?

### xix

Truth is, for instance, the rival actor, waiting, on the wings of a stage
for the appropriate cue,
or someone diving off a pier
into the dark-ringed water
from a signal arranged elsewhere.
Truth is not said.
Truth is the not-yet said.

Why do only bells make her cry?

Sound in the vacant silence, I suppose, the raising of nerves
held at times with those mundane acts,
at times with fairy tales, well-rehearsed function, the conventional talk
of an existence she's adopted in vaguely hostile territory.
Each Christmas, as she trims the tree, she leans in to listen to the radio.
Cologne,
the Dom, the Bell of the Three Kings (*Dreikönigsglocke*)

cast in the fourteen-hundreds she says.
It breaks the surface, the long
far-off jerk of metal ringing
and swinging its rippled swing.
Meanings loosen and lift like that.
It's not enough to make any of it real for us.
She reaches up into the abyss with a raffia star
like she could raise her homeland.

In private, words shape a wood around her.

Pine tree drying by the side gate,
brown of the dying needles,
hollowed trunk, bark.

I remember the scent hung helplessly in the air there for months.

My mother, her outsized Kassel shopping bag round her arm, comes in to the dining room perfectly dressed in a green silk outfit, her hair in a bun; she has a pocket prayer book in her hand, with bookmarked pages.

**xx**

I wrote,
*What about hopefulness?*
*Not long ago I loved you like a woman carrying a jug in a painting.*

And
*It is Paul Cox weather.*

I thought, all I want now is to be able to separate properly.

I thought, all I want now is rain falling rain
breaking the sky.

In my field of vision a late afternoon in summer.
A window of blackbird and blackbird and blackbird
and speckling trees.

Heat, lengthened shadows,
the cracked plastic compost bin gathering dust.

# In the Wind's Way

## Fritz Leonhardt
## The Baltic Sea, 1944

>'Oh God of Thymbra, grant a home
>And walls to weary men, grant us posterity
>And an abiding city; guard our second
>Tower of Troy, this remnant left alive
>By Danaan swords and pitiless Achilles.
>Whom should we follow? Or by what sea way
>Dost thou direct us? Where may we settle now?
>             – *Aeneid*, Book III: 120

### 11.43 p.m. 30 December 1944

And the sea at night shimmers tangled and dark with the bow of the ship
    rushing towards the Norwegian shore,
the mulch of turbine engines
    trailing tails of spume.

Inside the operations room the two NCOs,
    Fritz and Paul,
        exchange looks. And when the commander, lifting his gaze,

takes his seat, Fritz Leonhardt says to him
*Course set, Skagerrak Strait, north-west and steady*
    and braces, inhaling the stale air, attentive,
        (his black hair gummed stiff under his cap's rim)
though little arrows of worry pierce his ribs.

## 11.57 p.m. 30 December 1944

Distance holds hope, like a fiancée's postcard.

*LIEBER FRITZ*
*DER WINTER ist SEHR KALT. ICH BITTE GOTT*

*für IHRE SICHERE Rückkehr.*

## 12.02 a.m. 31 December 1944

On deck, Paul blinks at the cold, arms at his sides,
takes his bearings, and Fritz:
Fritz Leonhardt stands looking out,
not talking and looking.
Runs through what he knows. Count crew
along the rail, check the trade winds and trainees.
It's close to midnight: it's a great
sprawling of clouds with a horn
of moon,
and the turn of the world
can often be found at this hour.
You can see nocturnal seabirds scavenging,

you can see them in the ship's beam,
darting through
the waves' jagged rim, and in the netted
light of the whitecaps.

Fritz stands nice
and quiet. What comforts him is heavy steel cutting
through the water. Eleven hundred
      kilometres
at seventeen knots.

He glances between turret and metal grid out to a range
of open sea whose voice quickens as it heaves

and look –
two shearwaters
shrieking
sinking
feeding
as the liquid hills

are blown and tossed above the watermark, feeding, then wheeling into
    the dark:
and if he angles his eye up the column of the funnel, an oblong rising
    from a city of shapes,
a skyscraper splitting the wind, he can feel

an almost reckless calm
in his relation to the ocean on which
they cross,
high and glittering,

brackets and gaff points and dots
of cabin light, beads of incandescence, the colour of oxidised bronze,
and star pricks

coming through gaps in the rivets.
Sailing on,
passing through uncurbed waters, yet
who knows what goes on down there?

## 12.05 a.m. 31 December 1944

By this time, in his late thirties, all those thoughts have
moulded Fritz into someone who really only feels himself
    when thinking of someone else.
He continues to concentrate himself neatly
in the smaller spaces of his memory. He can turn his mind slightly
to veil some of the severity. A creative gift.

The years move very fast. He continues to neatly concentrate himself
    in the smaller spaces of his memory. In his head

    he carries fragments
so precious
        that the wounds attached have more of a scar quality –
        a kind of piecemeal arrangement of sensate images
painted from the inside. No,
        more like projected from the inside.
The living screen of a man's life, which sometimes shines
in the dark. What does he see? He has visions
that seem to forebode his death. As he stares
        out to the vast nothingness of the ocean, pictures
            quiver and dissolve, pouring out
through his black eyes.

## 12.06 a.m. 31 December 1944

Here's a family portrait: it is his mother in a silk brocade dress,
lace to her chin, book, pendant, wavy thick hair swept up, her gaze
        looking out in ringing silence; and there he is
with his sailor's collar
and his closed right fist, thumb hooked in the pocket
of his pleated trousers: in the formulations
        of husband/wife, brother/sister, they are obviously
        half a family – it's just the two of them –
but you can see how they're attached. And he is thinking

of his childhood, before the Führer and the NSDAP and the start of two wars,
        when the poppy daubed fields and pearly sky of August
seemed endless – before he realised the huge truth
of his sister's existence. Fine green shafts
of reeds lakeside. And the puffed tuftings of dandelion heads
        catching in the cracked stones,
and the trees' hollows and the jointed grasses swaying
alongside silted banks. *The best we can do*,
said his uncle – he was washing the scales from a
        Messer fishing knife with his usual stiff fastidiousness –

*is not retreat from life.* Fritz knew it was his mother
he was talking about: that his uncle had seen
The Whole Production
of her fall from what they termed
grace; that her generation had lived in a period of excess,
among the trappings of a prosperous city where liberal spirits caroused –
some in the inns, some on the Wegbereiter der Moderne, painters
and musicians from the newly sprung halls and art-houses
      rabelling through Chemnitz and Dresden and Berlin and
with all those acolytes swanning among them. Her slip of folly
had been to leave open the door to her room,
    or heart,
coming in from a performance of the Trout quintet with her eyes

'brushing the stars.' And the uncle who will tell him these kind of things
      periodically over the years
including the fact that she's never breathed the man's name
    in her life,
is a source from which further trickles
of information sometimes leak through.

*She has a lovely singing voice, of course,*
*she always did.* He folded two cleaned fish
in chequered cloth, placed them carefully in his fish box
then scooped out blobs of entrails from a wooden bucket
into a fresh-dug hole, soft and smelling of gravel. *She performed*
*in concert halls, parlours.* 'Some newer music perhaps,' *she'd say.*
'Yes,' Karl would say, 'But no one is happy without Strauss
and Volkslieder.' Sighed. Karl was the suitor
people had thought Most Likely To,
one of the few who remained a friend after The Whole Sorry Affair:
    a year later, conscripted into the Fourth Army,
        he'd be killed on a plain near Ypres.

*Sometimes we have good fortune,* his uncle said, *sometimes*
*we don't, but you have to understand we cannot escape*
    *from reality. It is tempting,*

*I know, to be mystic about things. And if not mystic,
romantic. But a time comes when eventually we have
           to take action. 'The joys of duty' and such,
which you've no doubt been told many times.*

*After a while, we inevitably pay for our experiences.
That's how it is. And I promise you, you save yourself a lot of trouble
if you're law-abiding, whatever else is said.* Raised the rim
of his hat. *You see* – regarded Fritz, head on a slight angle –
*how simple it would have been if she'd lived as women generally live.*
Shut the lid on the old fish box. *Her voice, you know,
is truly sublime.*

In the mornings from her room
           his mother singing –
this was Fritz's fantasy – light songs sung airily before the dresser mirror
           from some French or Italian operetta –
but in their flat any tune was swallowed.
He said something like *Won't she sing again
           when we've got more money?*
His uncle smiled. *It's possible. Though 'A man's manners,' Goethe said,
           'are a mirror in which he shows his portrait.'
And you know what is seen? Aloneness. Believe me,
there is no comfort
in being a law unto yourself.*

Something in Fritz folded its wings.
For perhaps the saddest thing about living without a father
is its premature instruction in the habits
of loss.
He felt as though he could slip his pain
between the little crevices of his ribs and out of sight, lining
the fleshed comb, the underside of his chest
with traces of love and hunger and shame.
He rotated his sorrow.
He looked away.
He was not a morose person;

but it made him hold back.
He knew what he had to do: elide, wait it out,

find ways to erect a boundary where he felt
    a core doubleness of self. *Above all else,*
    *don't let it show,* Helene once said.
Leni is his twin. When she spoke she had to be watched
    till her mouth stopped moving: he could see
glints of those other thoughts coming from underneath the conversation
like carp in the shallows,
    though eventually he came to feel her thoughts – something
not even her husband had learned –
ideas hidden behind the veiled glass of self that he sensed
from certain angles,
gestures of him and their mother showing in her forehead
    and lips, and marks developing from essential pigments and pictures
dividing and reproducing the shapes of past desires.

He lived with regulation, insinuated in him as it was
like the tendrils of vine into every crack and corner
of the dilapidated orphanage where he'd sought her out at fifteen.
    Regulation is what put him off knowing
what he should have known from the beginning. Yes, she stayed
in him. She came with directions that would forever keep all the action
offstage. On leave, he would cycle to meet her
    at the little island in the lake,
and sometimes he brought her home (with all that reflecting of the two
of them in the immense glaze of their mother's eye)
until he'd pulled out the stories and assembled the pieces and shown that
    they were really both sides of the same thing.
He had them photographed together. He sent her
Japanese silk. Fifteen years from now, when his uncle
has left his Pomeranian estate and moved west to Kiel.
    *I hear you found the sister. You never told me. And?*

## 12.12 a.m. 31 December 1944

Each thought weighs something.
The 2 a.m. call. (No personal calls till after 10 p.m.). Before his fiancée hangs up she will always say to him, praying the words into a promise,

*Ich bete zu GOTT*
*für ihre sichere Rückkehr!*

But what are the chances
he will return?

Distance is a stone with a string around it.

## 12.13 a.m. 31 December 1944

Fritz Leonhardt is a kind of cipher.
He transforms his own thoughts
through code. From things like his lowered centre of vision,

you can see each sign is what he makes it. Now
he's putting his hand in his pocket, curling his fingers
around his notebook.

It is leathery smooth, embossed in cursive groove on the cover,
*Tagebuch 1944*:
delicate as her, he thinks.

His heart is quickened by the feel of it. He traces the indentation, runs a finger along the cover's crevices. He knows the page he is up to –
it's the slight difference in the paper's texture, the pages

that have been opened and used, slightly soiled – and he
draws it out,
the drawing out of it connecting him

to the moment of putting it in
for the first time last December, which makes the twelve months
almost a circle, the year's

bracelet, when he'd made his way down as far as Chemnitz,
sitting in his mother's apartment
with his sister, his photography book,

his apple cake and lemon tea; the snow,
some afternoon sun in the window –
a milky monocle to the street…

## 12.19 a.m. 31 December 1944

On the morning of his enrolment with the merchant marine
Fritz tried to construct a future life from what was around him.
Detached from previous events he liked to think that here

he might belong, that there may be a way
      of locating himself
among the other fourteen-year-olds of imperfect means.
But on the morning of his conscription into the service

of the Third Reich, twenty years later, everything he'd built
fell away: because he was afraid
a chasm opened,

everything folded away, disappeared into the darkness
like an underexposed photo, because he wanted to be on a merchant steamer
      not the *Koln*,
because he was afraid.

## 12.22 a.m. 31 December 1944

      It's still long before dawn and as the chopping
        of the cold grey sea flicks shreds of ghostly foam
across the hull, as floes spit bits of ice in the air, Fritz
takes comfort from whatever steadiness he can find.

A roll of thunder turns on the horizon's brim, moonlight speckling
      the collarbone of the surf. Paul,
        legs solid as pegs, hands behind his back,
looks round. *I try remembering peace*, he says,

*and can't any more. He shifts, stretches,*
*thrusts the whole weight of his chest back into his shoulders.*
*I mean, even before, at sixteen, when we were in the on the skip*
Altona *and were scooped from the waters,*

*banned overnight by the British and flung into those internment camps in*
*New South Wales – that desolate place of either mud or dust –*
*I knew what the game was.*

Shrugs, heavy shadows
      on deck dragging under winter feet, *We've turned*
          *into a sporting nation,* he says, *and*
as you know, 'What is sport to the cat

      is death to the mouse.'

A silence spreads between them like landscape. And a slope of terraced cloud
      speeds in and bulges and blots out the stars,
         the petrels

            rising with heads tucked into the Romanesque curve
    of their arched wings, packed together and flying in a scuffle
from the waves into the fog as if to shear it to shreds,
while way off – so far there's no perceivable change in colour –
the skies continue to rumble in soft currents.

## 12.34 a.m. 31 December 1944

Fritz Leonhardt, who if he looks down, thinks,
if he looks out,
thinks – he is only a damned hair in routine's coat
but it's routine that keeps you alive –
      thinks – if he closes his eyelids
perhaps he will get a glimpse of the moment that is supposed to explain desire,
          explain vacancy. (For Fritz feels

his animal sense in constant movement,
though in his body, in his berth during rest hours, for instance,

       he will often find himself lying on his bunk –
  metal pipes and boiler uptakes cross-hatched, sleek under straining
lights, almost as if you could net the company –
thinking he is more of a hand-puppet animal really,
    a hand-puppet hare.

And then there are those blurred dreams, and then under them –
      it could be the yawning winds through the conning tower girders –
          the chill whispers of translucent
thrashed apart nothing.

He is used to switching registers.

Yet it's the way the emotional habits and fears, jostling,
rise and fall all at once. He'll even say to himself
there's solace in the berth's plainness.
         But there isn't solace there.

It mocks the idea of solace. It jostles the idea
with bits of galvanised certainty
the way a dormitory would if you were an inmate
    in an asylum
or government institution.) In the blackened winds
      the moon-streaked tower vanishes deep into tufts
        of oiling woolly cloud.

## 12.35 a.m. 31 December 1944

Fritz re-stabilises his hips and plants his feet.
Clenches his knees.
    What is beyond and behind the smouldering heavens?

So far. So long.

He is lock-jawed with apprehension.
His veins tug harder. He is bombarded by disturbances of thought
and with this formidable unreality makes himself someone

      whose want leaks from his skin like stuffing from a doll,

who is driven from a kind of sleeping existence through desire.

In the heart of the body of night,
of the yet-another future,
of broad blank water with history clamouring all across it, he stands
        exposed, looking out over the iron grey hill of the sea
to search for blackened wings
and shadows, and heat from the burning dreams
of the people who want to kill them.

An anxiety flows out of the bundled clouds and glides over the broad deck.

Hundreds of small eternities
come back to him. Dragonflies (abdominal segments
turquoise blue with black between each band
      like an Egyptian circlet)
hovering over the lake's green and greener fanned-out lily pads.
      Leni making her way to the edge of the water and holding out a hand,

long-limbed and light as gold. *What else is blood?*
    she had asked.
        *Doesn't consciousness come to mean the same thing,*

*a chance at getting what you want?*

Pointed boots, twisted protuberance of a willow root,
        duck shit.
      The smell of flour, grit, from when she'd had to bake
lebkuchen and tram dust flew in the windows that morning. Then laughing,

*Of course, I say this as someone who, by age eleven,*
*already had a feeling of life having passed them by.*

Fritz Leonhardt thinks about Leni being introduced to his fiancé,
kissing him on each cheek and whispering,
      *It will be all right, it will be all right,*
in her low serious voice. The autumn sun flowing over them.

## 12.59 a.m. 31 December 1944

As he walks towards the foremast, mists sprawling over
his face –

alarms. Silver knicks appearing in the fog
like claw marks in flesh.

Paul shouts from the bridge, We're set, and Fritz raises
    his eyes. In the distance
they hear the spun echoes of the real travel at speed
towards them. A minute from now the brass will say,
          *Everything you'll see you've been trained for,*
but these two seamen who have strengthened over years
as the bronzed warriors strengthened in the port of Aulis
are awash with numbness.
    What they'd give for this to be true.

    Thunder – they see a lone white bird in the flash
of lightning. They breathe air sharp
as a polished blade, they hold themselves
against the wind. Then the wind picks up, and low,
low, low, underneath it, long rumbling low, bit by bit, the growl
grows louder, and blows
right over the battle-lashed prow and like an airborne river rises
and runs, and flowing, rises and runs
into the hollows of the men's ears.

# Wasserturm (Water Tower)

### Gunnar Abt
### Berlin, November, 1934

> On the dark capes glisten
> Stains of ink and of wax.
> — Lorca

## Police Statement: response to Vorladung no: 378651.4
## Polizeipräsidium Alexanderplatz, Berlin 15.11.1934

On that Saturday in September,
we were happy to leave the city
but just as glad to get back.
In this story it's possible
to make a beginning and an end;
it should be understood, though,
the lines
are arbitrary.
What do you want to know?
There are always reasons
why things happen,
Willy Ziffen, our choirmaster,
likes to repeat
and is what he said
to us as usual
in the Romanische Café

the next day. Perhaps, it was his idea
of a joke.
Who can tell.
Marilee laughed
and her brother Hans, and my sister-in-law
Leni,
which is a rare enough occasion.
At any rate, we left the Schlachtensee
with the lake and woods
whispering violently
in our hearts,
a whispering, shall we say,
that seemed forged
from syllables of truth
and syllables of promise.
And on the train
Willy asked
whether it bothered us
what happened
with Buchrucker and von Schleicher,
talking about revolution
in soft hushed words
with the landscape running
across the window
as we headed into Berlin,
talking about revolution as if a song
had gurgled
like a stream from the bullet
in Schleicher's neck.
Yes, Rip off their tongues and
let them all bleed,
Erich said. And I recalled
how earlier that morning at the lake
we'd been singing from the old
Zupfgeigenhansl book,
*One quiet night before the light,*

and, All those knives in the night,
Erich had said, already drunk,
though he played his mandolin
with real feeling,
and Otto had his fiddle and Ulf
his guitar.
And the railroad car filled
with passengers from
Onkel Toms Hütte and Thielplatz:
we couldn't breathe
through all the cigarette smoke
and smells of
sweat and lavender, and
So what do you
think, my friends? said Willy.
The future is belief.
For we're in the ashes –
von Schleicher,
who was trying to rebuild
our defences, dead,
and his wife too –
such loss,
such ruin, Willy said,
from the corner of his seat;
I could barely see, but hung from him
on a rope of sound
until we arrived
at Prenzlauer Allee
and went out on to the street
which streamed with people
making their way home
from some Kraft durch Freude activity
of one kind
or another.
They looked sturdy
and energetic,

though occasionally you might see
a straggler, standing
in a doorway
like a straw ghost
aimlessly contemplating
the neighbourhood.
And after a draught of metropolitan life
in a couple of the bars,
where pleasure is worked
with sociability and delight,
worked by the girls too, done up
into little temptresses, a diversion
like dancing and cocaine that's to be found
everywhere these days,
we rolled
back out onto the pavement
where Ulf was sick,
which was unusual for him, in fact,
unusual in the sense
that as a professor of economics
at the Universität Unter den Linden,
he rarely miscalculates
on any front.
And with the rattling
of the trams
echoing in our ears,
we slid round into
Knaackstrasse,
where the strolling figures
shimmered under the lamplight,
and the damp air
produced by the light rain
fuzzed the avenue, making us
turn up our collars,
everything smelling
of stone

and felt.
And Willy, a government official
of higher standing
than me,
(I'm an accountant,
still making my way)
and someone better acquainted with
injustices and traitors
looked down the street,
which ran
narrow and flat
through the buildings
like the gap in a curtain,
and asked what we thought
of the thin young man
sticking a poster up
on the wall in front of us;
then went over
and shook the man by the scruff of the neck.
Repulsive communists, he said,
as he joined us again,
and we crossed into the park.
You could see the water tower
jutting out
above the trees,
very high, round,
and through some half bare branches
the dimly lit windows
glowing pale
and ghostly;
and Willy, smoking a cigarette,
was quiet suddenly,
pushing us past
the Schutzstaffel
guarding that tower camp
and along the path until we came out

onto Diedenhofer Strasse,
the expression,
tormented and washed-out,
of a drowned man
on his face.
How can we explain the despair?
The constant flow of it.
The despair that hungrily slurps
from your bowl,
that eats at your insides
and converts everything there to wind.
You could say, that evening in Prenzlauer Berg,
the old traces of despair rose
like vinegar from our stomachs,
like a faint aftertaste,
thin, but pointed in our mouths –
the lingering flavour of indignity
and injustice.
And when Erich talked
in a wheel of spiked frivolity
on what holds true and necessary,
the violations and procedures
of the immense enterprise,
and said weren't we pleased
with Germany's new style?
Willy was trying
to perk himself up
by nodding, mouth pulled
into a smile, but his eyes remained small,
watery blue: a sense of being
at the beginning of becoming human
made us think
we had to come through this heaviness,
this fogged up world, and this
suggestion that to understand anything
you had to proceed through life

as desperation demanded.
Weren't the sculptures of Arno Breker
infinitely more accomplished
than Barlach? Erich was saying.
And books uplifting,
purged of the dramatic effects
of treachery?
And after agreeing
we went on towards
Otto's apartment building
with rooks, starlings,
fluttering in nooks and alcoves:
the night around us
murmured with suppressed spirits,
alive and coming at you
like an invisible crowd:
we felt them walking with us,
Ulf and Erich discussing what is history,
Willy smoking,
Otto humming quietly to himself.
And I was thinking of Rosa –
I am in love, but not
with my wife,
of course – the fine young piece on the corner
had reminded me of a white bed,
bony ankles, a little balcony
opened
to the light.
A woman whose nails
are painted like raspberries,
who reads books
on Brazil and America,
and has pubic hair that spreads in tender curls.
And when she is asleep I am allowed
to stroke her feet.
More than anything I love

watching her put her housecoat back on;
and later, when I am home,
I wonder at how what looks so lovely
so ageless, like a gift
on her
can look so dowdy
on someone else.
And the clouds
over the roof lines
and the street
cast deeper shadows,
and the wind wrapped around our coats
and hair; and Erich
started to prod me
with his mandolin case and point,
and so we stopped
and read the newest bill
with regards to the reprisals
on Jewish businesses and betrayals.
We read, Insolent Jews have been arrested!
National Socialist Germany
demonstrates against World Jewry and its allies!
What goes around, comes around, we said.
And Otto wished us goodnight,
and we made our way slowly
along the pavement
to the corner.
And Ulf was perfectly
relieved again.
He wooed us with a gentle song.
And, Should we perform in the Winter Festival? asked Willy,
which Erich had raised,
picking at the strings of his instrument
with his enormous hands
on the lake
that morning.

And our heads turned on matters
of music,
and dreams
swimming up
like trout from the deep,
where stealth is tipped and tumbled
in slips
of lucent bronze: radiant glimpses
trailed
amid the fathomless dark.
Art, said Erich.
Culture.
Though I'm not much for
that talk.
Everything is largely calculation, I find.
And then we saw Willy,
approach the man
putting up a poster on the wall.
And we realised
it was the same man
we'd seen earlier.
He was pasting
indecent placards,
interfering with
the peace and quiet,
observing his work
with his head tilted at an angle.
So our little bit of suspect action, you see,
sprang from one: the shameful,
two: the incomprehensible;
and the groan
of a city disembowelled
over and again for years.
We watched Willy,
silhouetted against the gloom,
stick his revolver into the man's neck

and shoot him. Because
too often we're scrapped, Herr Officer,
not used or included,
carried by the wash
of this sweeping tide,
floating and being buffeted,
forbidden and no longer forbidding,
bystanders in your organisation,
Herr Officer,
your organisation that has admirable enough aims
and which we've longed to be part of
each day then
and each day
still long to be part of,
like fishermen without their oars
carried into the mudflats and shallows,
drifting towards the shingle,
feeling weather
come in from the west
but not yet able to see it,
like calves at the mercy of an early frost,
like puppets in the dark
behind the curtains,
Herr Officer,
carried by the ignominy
of external forces,
carried by the winds
of reproaches and inexpressible melancholias,
pulled-apart pilgrims
on relentless waves
of crap,
of lies,
the spectres of your republic.
For a moment Willy
looked down
with unchanged expression.

And then someone shouted, SS!
and they came forward
and saw our victory for order and for the dead
still among us.
And we began singing, *Gute Nacht Mutter*.
And our hands were raised.

This water tower in Berlin was the first recorded concentration camp in Germany.

# Dear Sister

## Christof Henriks
## Hamburg, May 1970

> How then, leaving the mountains,
> Content with German lands he calmly
> Moves on and stills his longing
> In useful industry
>
> – Hölderlin

It has taken a little longer than I'd have hoped to send my Easter wishes, forgive me! As usual, it was a very busy time, and you know how tied up I get at school with marking papers and so on. In the end, though, it was an interesting visit that we made to Berlin for the holidays with the children, travelling through some nice stretches of countryside, then meeting up with Gunnar, Marilee and the family. The weather was completely clear and once we'd got past the border guards – who wouldn't let the children laugh and even poked mirrors under the car to check we weren't hiding anything! – it was a very pleasant, smooth trip. Again, what a wonderful city. (Or half of one anyway!) Just the museums and bookshops were enough to keep us occupied for the week. We took walks through the Tiergarten. Saw trees with green shoots. The bison statue. Our hotel was barely a kilometre away. (Having been to the zoo last time, we were able to avoid spending hours looking at animals that really should be elsewhere and free.) We heard Claudio Arrau play a terrific concert at the Philharmonie (Bartok, Brahms.) We also had dinner with friends of Gunnar's, who live in a lovely big top floor apartment on Kantstraße. She is a doctor. He's a translator, French, likes to quote from Baudelaire, which was mostly directed at his son, a young man who considers himself a socialist. After eating, I went out on the balcony with G and his friend, looked out over the city lights, and his friend produced three glasses and a bottle of Rémy-Martin cognac. As you've observed I'm not much of a drinker, but even I could appreciate that this was something special. Ewald spent most of the time with his head in a book of some kind or other, and I am happy to say the same can now be said of his younger brother. His loves are crime and mystery stories, the Martin Beck series, Agatha Christie, that sort of thing. How are you and Bernard and the growing tribe? And what is the latest situation with Bern's health? Of course, I am hoping it is not too long before we see each other again. If only Melbourne wasn't so far. Distance is so troublesome! Are you finally getting a bit of help from the children?

# The Masurian Lakes

### Hans (and others)
### Prussia/Poland, June 1945

> Slowly Death is singing.
> – Döblin

*Everything turning to slush, while he must drag his feet each day
to Leningrad, though when he sleeps
whatever's there is blotted out by pictures
of the house where he lived, in Niedergörsdorf we've heard,
unless there's been too much mould in the bread
and his stomach won't let him rest.*

*An old soldier of fifty, sixty years,
doesn't he know they'll use any excuse
to kill him? Who hasn't seen the men in the countryside
laid out in thorns and loneliness, heels pointing to heaven, their limbs
stiff in the earth? And we're no different. These waters too,
will take whatever's given.*

**returned veteran of the First World War,
captured member of the Volkssturm, Jüterbog**

Hell, I'm tired, doomed, that's a fact. I've lived as if being slowly encroached by a sewer. I've watched the boys I know destroyed, boys whose parents made their livings like most villagers, selling eggs and growing vegetables and clearing the forests. Boys who believed prosperity would pass over the land like a perfect sun-soaked day and fill them with happiness. For five years, a glass eye from the last war kept me from the trenches, but eventually I had to put on my old First World War uniform when I was drafted too. Kids, cripples, everyone's had to give their all. And now, here we are, a gift from the Americans to the Soviets: we'd have rather set our fate with the Ammies, but they handed us to the Red Army out of solidarity and friendship. Really, I'm a ghost, but still not without fear. I tramp in boots warped and cut by months of snow and ice, the bitter breeze across the lakes constantly ruffling my beard, a breeze that carries the smells of still water and fish and rotting reeds and flesh, and too often I think I'd prefer a quick brutal end to this slow march to non-existence. Only occasionally do I dream of release. Yes, sometimes a voice inside urges me to keep on going, because if I don't keep on going I'll die on the road and then the crows will devour me. I'll die on the road by some swamp, black rain clouds passing over me, a sack of bones splitting goose-blue skin. And the Russians will leave me there nameless. They'll march on.

*He's rolling on the balls of feet*
*to get his balance, clutching clumps of grass*
*on the bank, and when he nears the top*
*a fellow prisoner hauls him up*
*gripping his wrists with both hands*

## Emil, a sculptor and Wehrmacht conscriptee, captured outside Jüterbog

Yeah, I know what you mean. I guess we all did things, said things, we now have to forget. During those years, we didn't want to dangle. That's war, I suppose; the regrets must come later. To my girl, it was crazy from the outset. She thought I wouldn't survive a week. We didn't see each other as often as we'd have liked because she was a dancer and worked at night and while I was doing my military training I was still getting commissions for my sculptures. They included requests from committee members for schools and public buildings, famous figures I had to knock out, poets, and musicians et cetera, but what they also wanted were nudes, perfect examples of the Aryan race, nude male figures, but female figures too, which are certainly sweet to make. I used to get my girl to model. The sculptures were a tribute to her and stood for the beauty of women everywhere, and made their way into the homes of Sergeant Walder and Einsatz leader Beutzog. Also restaurants and parks in Schöneberg, Charlottenburg, Mitte and Potsdam. But then one day she comes round, says she's sick of being recognised, sick of people knowing what she looks like undressed from having seen my work. Emil, she says, stick to dead geezers and dogs. After I was assigned to the Ninth Army's Light Infantry Division I never saw her again. A letter, a pair of socks, and a notebook turned up the day before my departure – by what she wrote, it was clear she thought I was never going to make it.

*Kosemühl, Willkassen, Neurode, our vast*
*spreading lagoons floating and wavering*
*and coursing into one another*

## Axel Kirsch, Wehrmacht Infantry Fourth Army Division 156, captured at Kreuzberg station, Berlin

Do you know Marga Schoeller's bookshop? I went there every morning to browse the English literature shelves. It's a fine bookshop. One of the best in Berlin. You can spend your whole day there without having to buy anything. Everything is set up in such a way that you move from one pleasure to the next. I generally started with theatre or American poetry. If it was after an early shift, one of the girls would bring me coffee and cake. They were both blonde, which is neither here nor there, though I always hoped it was the tall, snobbish one that was working that day who'd bring me the library ladder, point out the latest arrivals, rather than her short, plump, cheerful colleague, two or three years younger. There was something vaguely distasteful about the older one, her white body, icy stare, the air of disappointment that clung to her, which I found perversely appealing: she had the gravitas and composure of an erotic malcontent. And she'd read all of Virgil.

One morning, while I was searching for a copy of Eliot poems, I noticed that a thin booklet was lying folded and wedged behind the books. Tugging the pamphlet out in curiosity, I found it was a collection of pornographic photographs, not particularly sophisticated or stylish, just pictures along the usual lines, naked women with their backs to you, or draped in nothing but strand of pearls alongside a fully clothed man, or sitting in armchairs with stockinged legs splayed. Before I'd managed to stuff the booklet back where I'd found it, the younger girl came up next to me and said something, a gravelly voice speaking in Saxon dialect, as if she knew what I'd just seen, although she looked at the section where I was standing and, Prufrock? she said. That's a back order we're still waiting on.

For a moment, we stood looking at each other – suddenly even the tousled greasiness of her pinned hair seemed provocative – and I didn't know what to do.

Blushing slightly, she slipped a rough, reddened hand in among the books – I'm not sure why her hands were like that; perhaps she had a second job washing dishes – taking the pamphlet out, flipping through it and then looking back at me, her clear, green-eyed gaze unwavering, or perhaps not unwavering, but strong, not at all like someone who had no idea of passion, the possibilities of sex, and then she turned away – and I'm following her.

Here, I say, pulling her through the red curtain that divided the shop from the office. She knows I've slipped the booklet into my pocket. Dance for me, I say. She's a sweet girl, but she won't dance, give me that pleasure. She smiles awkwardly in a way that displays her crooked teeth. Her mouth is damp and open. How old are you? I ask. Eighteen, she says. Go on, dance for me, I say. No, she says, laughing and leaning back on the desk. What should I do? What does she want? The shop is empty, so I swivel her round and press against her rear in one motion. And when I do she stiffens, from surprise I suppose, and I lift her skirt and rest my hands on her hips and dip in. Dip, dip, dip, I keep on going. The girl moves rhythmically, and I'm watching her bare neck, a small purple bruise on her neck, I'm watching her and she knows I'm watching her. It's this connection I'm hungry for. So we fuck, excited by the energy the connection generates, and about the fucking. Then I've finished, and she straightens, turns and looks at me again, The pictures belong to my colleague, she said; she has a girlfriend and prefers women anyway.

We talked for a while, about Robert Frost and Heine, and then I said goodbye and left. And that was it. I never touched her again, though sometimes I still think about her, see her standing there with her straggly hair and soft neck, imagine I can smell the faint vegetal smell of her. And you know what? It's the booklet, not Virgil or Eliot, that I now keep with me day and night.

## Kurt, a Werwolf guerrilla, captured at Charlottenburg, Berlin

Well, go on, go on, show us what you're talking about, won't you? It's been a long time since I saw a naked woman, in the flesh or in a book for that matter. And these are the best kind of books in my opinion. These are the only books I want to see. Before being captured, I was actually in love with a girl in Nauen, an art student from Potsdam. I can't remember how we met, but she moved in with a couple of my friends and one night we talked and kidded around till five in the morning and ended up in bed. She was, I have to tell you, very good-looking, really pretty, educated, big breasts. Kurt, she says, you can screw me, but don't trust me. And of course, I wanted to know what made her say that. Because, like you, she says to me, I'm attracted to – well, let's call it the spirit of resistance. So I had to drop it there. I took it she was up to some sort of covert thing too. Occasionally, of course, we had disagreements. It was me usually, wanting stupid things, like to fuck her in the arse. Man, it's impossible to find anyone apart from whores who'll go for that. But our endless lovemaking kept us more than happy, and when there was a successful sniping or sabotage against the allies, for example, we'd shut the blinds, smoke a cigarette, ask each other what we'd heard about, what had been hit or how many had died, just general information, you know, questions that carefully avoided anything that could any way be construed as suspect, and we'd roll over and touch each other again, and keep touching and have sex again, and we'd laugh a lot and were silly, but all the time we had an absolute idea of how we wanted the world to look by the time we were thirty I can tell you, no misunderstandings there.

This was a good war for me, you know, *ganz prima, ganz prima*. And, let me tell you, it would be a huge mistake to assume all is done and we're lost. There's no way it's finished yet. I've learnt a few things and nothing's what it seems at first glance and it may be a long road, but things will be put right. The allies won't be here forever. No, no way. Let me tell you, it's not over, believe me.

*What we hear now*
*we hear from many of them –*
*a lack of food turns passion*
*into desperation. For three months, this young vigilante's*
*way through fear and hunger has been remembering.*
*He is providing his own sustenance.*
*It is a function of deciding how well*
*you want to survive… To open his throat is, in any case,*
*to do something. The words issue*
*from his mouth and tumble over the stones*
*and pebbles on the road into Russia,*
*onto the piles of fallen snow,*
*onto the vast expanses of the cleared fields,*
*onto the sodden earth of the black woods,*
*onto the swaying grasses, the swollen pools*
*of melted ice, the crocuses and the foamy drifts,*
*onto the whole array of military personnel and devices.*
*He wants to be brave forever*

## Kurt, Waffen SS volunteer, captured from a field hospital outside Königs Wusterhausen

My father had one and a half arms. He lost the bottom of his right arm in a farm accident, adjusting the rotor blades on the motorised plough. My mother got cancer just after war broke out. She was in and out of hospital, which at least taught us to cook meals and wash our own clothes. In 1942 the war was still going well for Germany, so I volunteered for the SS. Back then, it was like I was preserving my family's honour. I had my little brother to help with the farm and we could do with the money. I wasn't the only one. There were dozens of men in a similar situation in the district and we wanted to be part of the Reich, get on board.

Initial training was three months and from there I was stationed at Treptow, twenty miles south-east of Berlin. When the Russians moved close to the area, I arranged it so that I was put in reconnaissance – I've ridden motorcycles since I was ten, still even have a Zundapp 750 under covers in the barn – and I went out and kept watch, gathering information on routes taken or flank protection operations, which as the war went on became harder and harder; nobody really knew where the front lines were any more.

By the end of December '44, coal and oil, the Reich's lifeblood, had virtually dried up. The ice and snow were too bad for riding anyway, and I was ordered to take a machine gun and set up in the trenches with the other gunners. One day I was on a bunker about a hundred metres away behind headquarters and an officer shouted, 'The Russians are coming!' and all of a sudden there were bullets and shrapnel exploding everywhere around us. It took more than sixteen hours to pitch for what we thought was the front line. Fragments of bodies splattered over heads: it was like rain on the metal of our helmets. Then we ran out of ammunition and the fighting stopped. We didn't know what to do next. I thought we'd see the Russians come out in droves roused by their success. But once it was over, all you really saw were the corpses, some lying across the road almost like they were asleep, some furrowed and flattened beyond recognition where the tanks had run over them.

After we'd surrendered, I was picked out and taken to First Aid – for the hole in my cheek and I hadn't even realised I'd been wounded – and from there stuck in one of their field hospitals, which in terms of survival meant that your chances, if you were lucky, were enough for them to give you a bit to eat before they sent you to a slave labour camp; but the medical care was atrocious. The pain inside my jaw still tears through me day and night, and you can see where I've got part of my face missing obviously, as well as a number of teeth.

Each day at dawn you were made to get up and go outside, supposedly for exercise, but in reality it was so they could check to see how far off you were from being able to be put to work. One day we were even marched to a kind of clearing, it was like a picnic spot, where the Russians had brought all the Jews from one of the camps. They'd been put there to jeer and humiliate us as we trudged through. When we tried to sing a patriotic song or anything the reprisals were hideous. The Ivans would kick you to the ground, tramp on your head, let anyone do whatever they felt like if it made you the butt of ridicule.

But I'm keeping a record of all this. The whippings, the shootings, the miles we've marched, every place en route, the butchering, dismembering, victims who've had their eyes ripped out, genitals mutilated; and the rank and identifying features of the perpetrators. They're grotesque, out of control, bandits, rapists. I haven't got my blood type tattooed under my arm for nothing – though sometimes I think I should have been smarter, pretended to be one of those scientists who's an expert on chemicals, or rockets, or has a special formula, can turn anything into anything, that the Americans are begging for and carting off in truckloads. If only we'd smashed the 4th Guards' tanks – they moved in so fast – but our resources hung by a thread. In fact, we were outnumbered, and as a result ended up in a bloodbath. High Command let us down, not the SS, or the Wehrmacht. We never lost sight of things.

And now, what about these ridiculous instructions, these ridiculous lessons in how to be Communist the Russians keep giving us? If it weren't so tragic, it would be funny. They might think they're having some effect, but what they're demonstrating is their spectacular ignorance, their stupidity. I can barely stop my astonishment getting in the way of my disgust. It makes me sick to the stomach, not that there's anything in there anyway, being starved to death as we are. Some days I feel so crazy I could kill myself. But I don't want to give them the satisfaction.

*You can see hope passing*
*like the seasons.*
*That is how we mark time.*
*A summer tourist, for example, stepping*
*from the dock to his boat*

*smells the sun on his skin.*
*His pupils sizzle in this light.*
*Way. Out. There, he says*
*His voice drifts across the white drenched*
*surface – daylight licking the water –*
*and even through the cotton of his starched shirt*
*he feels his back burning. He stops, he thinks*
*he drinks. He unwinds the rope*

*and tosses it to one end,*
*pushes the boat from the jetty.*
*Water cracks apart*
*like a soft plum.*
*There is a soft arhythmic sound as he settles*
*on his suede cushion,*
*slapping this way and that against the boards.*
*He rows to the lake's centre.*
*Drops a hand over the side*
*drawing trails behind him*
*and visualising tiny fish rushing*
*into the depths. They are flickering through*
*a weedy current – shiny – slimy – tiny*
*tender bodies streaming in the*
*waves waves waves waves waves*

*and then he stands, undresses, dives in.*
*Dives in, swims,*
*his arms forging little windmills*
*and flinging bits of silver light through the*
*waves waves waves graves waves*

## Hans Henrik, technical engineer, captured at Jüterbog Luftwaffe base

My story? My father was an industrialist. After he died, my brother and I took on the business. Of course, the years leading up to the war were profitable for me. There was an increase in production of cement pipes and copper lines at the request of the government, an obligation to assist with national development.

Then in 1939 one of us had to join up. Neither wanted to go, but in the end I was sent to work as a supervising engineer at an airfield near Berlin. I've been creating monitoring and operating systems, adjusting turbines, compressors, pressurisation, cooling systems, hydraulics, anything that's needed in the Arado Ar 68s, Focke-Wulfs, Henschels and Messerschmitts used by the Bf 110 and Fw 190 squadrons, which has allowed me to maintain position as someone who doesn't kill. I'm a God-fearing man. Yet I'm struggling now to understand what rules apply to me, and God, and everyone. See, here's a photo of my son, my daughter, with Leni, my wife. More fragile, more delicate than many, she's been digging trenches with her bare hands, at least eight to ten hours every day, among other futile reasons because she'd be shot by our own men if she wasn't prepared to accept her patriotic duty. Worse than that was my fear that she'd be taken for a Jew – she's dark, and I was worried that one day we'd have to prove it, although I'm certain she's not. Thing is, though, she's illegitimate, brought up by the state. One of twins, apparently her mother couldn't afford to keep her. Before she was a year old, she was packed off to a string of orphanages and foster carers, and her hometown has since been bombed and the papers lost.

Of course, you can spend years talking about If only *this* and If only *that*. It's the shock of the reality of defeat. There are those who'll argue for hours about the advantage lost after Dunkirk in staging parades rather than surging ahead, the chaos of Goering's air procedures. But it's useless, isn't it? The tables have turned. And although my heart can only dimly bear it, now we've been driven back I am filled with a terrible portent that these Russians will fell our wives and children as surely as they hunt beasts...

*Swaying on their heels. One foot*
*in front of the other.*
*Their activity is reduced*
*to this, just one foot in front*
*of the other.*
*These men are not*
*familiar with this land.*
*Place names have changed. And will*
*change back again.*
*All through the war the forests*
*to north and east*
*were marked as part of the wooded plains*
*of Augustow on their maps.*
*Names they were able to comprehend,*
*Rastenburg, Allenstein, Zichenau,*

*Lötzen they'll be surprised
to hear as Kętrzyn, Olsztyn
Ciechanow, Giżycko.
Wilamowo's X-shaped airstrip
is rent. While nearby
what was the 'Wolf's Lair'
sinks its weighted decay
and shrouded fortifications
made from concrete and hoisted trees
into the forest floor.
The matted shadows
expand amid the earth and foliage
as if in readiness. As if saying to the dead souls*

*of Stauffenburg and his officers, people
are all the same and one day
these men too, will disappear between
the sunlight and the craggy earth,
between the shallows and the seeping earth,
between the grasses
and the cold earth.*

*Now comes the wind,
and the clouds bring rain across the forest
and on the heads
of the captives and guards.
The men go seeking shelter under the canopy,
but the guards empty their mouths
like open beech hollows*

## Sergei, squadron commander Soviet Union armed forces, 1st Belarusian front

What do you think you are doing? Where do you think you are going? Получить там! we've said. Get back! We've seen you kill off battalions with your pockets full of papers, seen you stack icy holes full blood-matted souls with indifference. Mercy reflects the cowardice of a poor memory. That is, make one wrong move and you're finished!

## Nils Klaubach, Wehrmacht conscriptee, Infantry Division 158, captured at Luckenwalde

Huh, do they think their threats, or the rain will trouble me? My wife died when the British bombed Magdeburg in January. I've lost two sons and a daughter too. One son in a U-boat somewhere in the western Baltic, one in Narvik. My daughter died in the air raid on Hannover. Her two-year-old son died with her. The only relative I've left is her baby girl, who was found quite calm in her upturned cradle.

And what was I doing during this war? Until I was drafted in March I was simply an administrating official in a government organisation, assisting in the allocation of departmental labour and services. I hadn't picked up a rifle. I wasn't even a party member. The Americans and the Russians attacked and attacked and we Germans were afraid, weren't we? We were desperate and we prayed.

All winter long, the thunder of battle had galloped closer to the town. There were American planes overhead and the sound of Russian artillery in the hills. Refugees were pouring through from the east from our territories in Prussia, but also from Poland, Sudetenland, Romania, Hungary. Panzer Groups were formed, and I was in charge of ordering replacements. Everyone was given a Panzerfaust, that cheap portable anti-tank warhead, barely more than a grenade on a stick to my mind, the so-called people's weapon. Fifteen million pieces had been manufactured the previous December and distributed amongst the Volkssturm, although most had little clue how to use them properly and were actually frightened of them.

By February, new orders were coming through every day. Then, one night, I was given the command to take into custody any person who was evading his summons into the service. It seemed we had more deserters than anywhere for a hundred miles.

At first light, the local division commander, who kept his cattle behind the police station and rode his horse through the district every Sunday after church, came into my office in his high polished boots, flinging a box of record books on my desk and barked at me, Attend to this immediately, is that clear? He laid a wad of printed sheets on the table in front and spent a minute running over the names with me, then stormed off into the icy street.

Outside on the main street of the town, dingy as a funeral, the local police and several soldiers from the sixth unit of the 588th Division were assembling. Grey clouds dissolved across the buttermilk sky. Children played in the stoops, coughing. The recent air raids on nearby Magdeburg and the district's synthetic oil plants had filled the air with smoke, making it hard to breathe, and many of the town's folk were sick, plunged into a record-breaking cold winter without sufficient means for heating, and there wasn't enough food to get them back on their feet, as you'll remember, and we were surrounded by cases of pneumonia, sometimes treated, if we had supplies, but more often than not people relied on brandy to fix the problem. Sometimes the pitiful wheezes and uncontrollable hacking robbed even a card game of the capacity to deliver its bit of relief from the fear and boredom. I looked at those coughing children playing with flags and paper planes, and wondered if anyone really gave a damn. But who knows, maybe I was already living in the realm of the dead. I'd slipped away from the person I once knew as myself, at any rate.

The soldiers and police nominated the areas they would search. I told everyone they had to regroup in my office at the end of the day and inform me of their progress, complete the necessary documents. They set off. I decided to begin on the northern outskirts of town myself. I wondered what sort of reaction there'd be from those brought in. There were names I knew among them on the list. I knew they were just scared, for they were mostly old – Kurt Glaub, the ex-fire chief, Sebastian and Gert Hoffmann, retired railway workers – men aged or affected by debilitating conditions.

Glancing through the list, I thought I'd start by looking up Hans Teichmann, a teacher I'd had years ago at school, and who, by this point, I imagined was around sixty. Resigned, somewhat despondent, I got in my car and drove towards where he lived on a small farm. His house with its bony wooden back slumped tiredly against the hill. I remember I felt as if there was something of an aura of brooding decay about it and in the surrounding landscape. Perhaps he'd perished from pneumonia, I thought to myself. The vehicles squeezed between the pines left wet, dark stripes in the snow. It was bitterly cold.

I drove up the drive to the front of the house, knocked on the Teichmann's door, and, Mrs Teichmann, I said to his wife, stepping through without waiting to be asked, is there a reason your husband hasn't obeyed the law?

He's sick in bed, she said. She pointed down the hall with a finger.

Surely, I said, you're aware you must notify the authorities?

For an instant she looked at me as if she didn't recognise what language I was speaking. I told her to stay where she was and went into the bedroom. I called out for Mr Teichmann, but he didn't seem to hear me. He was lying face-up, very stiff and under a mound of covers, like the sarcophagus of a medieval knight. From the lack of colour of his face and the burning in his eyes, I could tell he was, in fact, dying.

After making a brief report in my notebook, I went back out to his wife. If what you say is true, you must get a certificate from the doctor immediately, I said. How else can I prevent the Gestapo from taking him in?

She nodded, without raising her head, and I went out and got back in my car.

During that day, I visited nine addresses in the region. Despite my best efforts, apart from Hans Teichmann I only managed to find two of the names we were looking for, a boy of seventeen and his sixteen-year-old cousin, who had joined the Hitler Youth and apparently set their minds on fighting, but whose parents no longer accepted there was any hope that the war could be won. In my heart, I believed they were right, the war was lost, but I was driven by the nature of my character and the duties I was there to fulfil. I took down the required information, and told the lads what would happen if they didn't report the following morning: they would be charged, in short, and thrown into prison. I advised them to pack their bags that night and then returned to town.

When I got to my office, I found a number of deserters had been apprehended and were being held in the police cells. They were waiting for the arrival of the truck that would take them to the camp in Magdeburg where they'd be joined to one of the existing units. I thought about the two boys. There was no more guarantee they'd turn up the next day than when they were supposed to have, a fortnight earlier. I knew I'd been too lenient, hadn't dealt with the problem as strictly advised. I have to say I wasn't surprised when at half past four the local unit commander came into my office and gave orders for me to return immediately and fetch the young men – young men, it was clear, he said, who hadn't understood the potentially disastrous consequences of their behaviour, since there was absolutely no tolerance by the military or SS of cowardice, or dishonour, or whatever anyone wanted to call it.

This time, I was accompanied by the chief of police and one of his officers. In the headlights on the narrow stretch of road back to the farm, I noticed the black branches of the bare trees swaying in the wind, the icy reeds by the stream lashing the bank, snow in the hollows. And it began sleeting again. The police chief and his officer talked and joked with one another. I had no interest in joining in.

It was after seven when we reached the boys' place. The house was quiet.

The police chief banged his fist on the door and his officer walked around to the rear, calling out, Answer! Answer the door! and at last a woman appeared.

There's no one here, she said, Only me. Shrugging, she informed us the children were in bed and the older boys at a crisis meeting for potato growers in the town hall.

It seemed pathetic that she should be so naive in the face of our showing up – I was dejected by the inevitabilities of which she was so blindly unaware, the poor level of her acting skills, the flush of her blood beneath the dry, wrinkled skin. I looked at the young officer, unimpressed.

They're determined to screw us, he said.

At dawn the next day, the three of us returned to the farm. But when we got there, it appeared there'd been a change of heart and the boys were in the kitchen with their Hitler Youth uniforms on and their breakfast in front of them. I told them we would leave as soon as they'd finished eating.

They agreed, and the police chief said, That's what we want to see, young men ready to serve our leader and our country, and they nodded and ate their rolls with lard.

For a while we waited, no one saying anything.

Then the police chief said, All right, enough, and went behind the older boy's chair, pulled the back out from under him so that he was forced to get to his feet. At this, the woman – who was his aunt or mother, I wasn't sure which – jumped across from the stove in the direction of the chief of police as if she might tear the hair from his head. He grabbed her hands, but she shook him off, then looking him directly in the eye, said she had something to tell him. Something more important than sending kids in to do battle.

Agitated, impatient, he said to her, Yes?

She said she knew where two Jews were hiding. She told us she'd reveal the spot if we promised that her son and nephew would be placed somewhere away from the fighting.

The police chief demanded to know if what she'd told us was really true.

Yes, she said.

He asked, Can you locate the Jews right now?

They've already evaded two searches, she answered, but it's a matter of knowing where to look.

To get some idea of her will to help, and her will for preservation, I asked her to name the location then and there.

As long as you give your word of honour, I'll tell you, she said, and I agreed I'd do what I could, assuming she'd understand that there were limits to my powers.

She gave me a calculating look, made me swear to it, got the chief of police and his officer to do the same thing and then, taking us into the front parlour, gestured through the window at the neighbouring property, the Teichmanns' property, which, as I've said, I'd investigated myself, only the day before.

We're going to take the lads with us, said the police chief, and if it's as you say, we'll promise to do our best to keep them at the home front.

According to her, the Jews were hidden in the Teichmanns' hay barn. We drove across to the farm and I went into the house while the police chief and officer searched the barn. The two boys remained in the car. The house was as I'd left it the day before, just my old teacher, breathing his last, and his wife cooking soup. I went and joined the others, but they were unable to find anything. The barn was musty and dark, the roof leaked. As a gesture of solidarity, I got the boys out of the car and directed them to the loft, and they threw around straw, pulled at the timbers, kicked wood shavings to the floor; but there was nothing of interest unearthed, no sign that anyone was there.

We turned to leave. I let everyone know we'd be heading straight into town. Then from the shadows we heard a noise, which stopped me in my tracks. At first I thought it was birds in the rafters. But the others had heard it too. A woof, sort of muffled, as if someone were trying to stifle a cough.

The officer went over to a dilapidated hay wagon in the corner. He threw aside the layers of straw and leaves to find there were some loose boards concealing a false bottom. The Jews, a man and woman, a couple I took to be roughly in their early twenties and married, lay clutching each other as insects crawled away from the light. Everyone gazed into the hay wagon somewhat dumbstruck, except the police chief who went over and levelled his pistol.

I didn't know what procedures I was meant to follow in this kind of situation. I went back to the house. I put a call in to headquarters. Mrs Teichmann said she didn't know a thing about any of it and I told her we'd deal with her later. The policemen marched the Jews to the car, while the boys stood some distance behind. The Jews were both very thin, particularly the woman; at one point, I watched her coughing till she could barely stand. The head of police held his nose, told her she was too diseased to travel in the same vehicle with us. He told the two of them he would leave his officer there to guard them and to return to the barn and kneel facing the wall: they stumbled across together and knelt there like that, arms behind their heads.

Do we come with you? one of the boys asked me.

Of course, I said. Hurry up, will you. Get in the car.

The boy who'd spoken did as instructed. But before the rest of us were in the car, his companion took off, running across the fields towards his house on the hill. Naturally, the police chief charged off across the field after him. I watched, thinking in all likelihood he'd soon overtake the boy, yet I was worried about what might happen if the boy did threaten to disappear from sight. I knew the chief's temper was on a short fuse and that he might make some sort of drastic move. But that's the risk the boy took, I suppose. And when he neared the crest of the hill, the police chief drew out his pistol and shot in to the air. The boy stumbled and fell. The police chief reached him, leapt on him, dragged him up by the scruff of the neck, then marched him back to the car, where I was now waiting in the driver's seat. Forced to the ground in front of the vehicle, the boy lay there, panting, while the police chief went into the barn, reappearing not long after with a coil of rope slung over his shoulders and a piece of plywood under his arm. Before hanging him from the tree at the front of the driveway, he wrote a placard which he strung around the boy's neck. 'I am a deserter. I have failed to defend the German people and must die.' I stayed in the car, my head spinning, and there were pains running down my shoulders and I felt ill.

The head of police told the remaining lad, who was crying, that he was delivering him directly to the Magdeburg camp. The decision was made to take the Jews at the same time after all. I'd wanted to go across to let the woman know about her dead boy, and I said as much to the policemen, but they'd objected. They were both exhausted. I drove us quickly into town, although the Jews were a problem I still didn't know how to solve.

As we came over the bridge, a Volkssturm brigade sat and smoked at the end of the main street. It was strangely quiet. When the police deputy had taken the Jews and locked them in a cell, his superior sent for a car and driver, telling them to get the boy to camp. I then went to my office, filled out the paperwork, had a brandy and took an aspirin.

So, you see, I didn't have a comfortable life. I wasn't top brass or a staff general. I was a civil official, relatively low in the chain of command. Night after night I had problems sleeping. Wasn't I doing my best? What else could I have done? I worked hard, defended our regulations with zeal. I didn't try to stand aloof from responsibility. Europe was our problem! War is war, and I had a family to consider! If it wasn't them, it would be us. And I did my best, I tell you. My best.

*Yes, there are past gifts of battle*
*the old wooden bridges, the medieval kingdoms,*
*so many things like this*
*disappearing within the lake basin.*
*When war struck last time they would drop*
*their mines into the flat water, lying*
*like a drum skin under the spumey sheen*
*of the September sky*

*and ride away: and we would cool*
*and encompass*
*and steadily pull anything that let itself*
*be pulled out of sight. It's not easy to draw lines:*
*the crabs crack, the terns drown,*
*the dinghy creaks, the foundations muddy,*
*the moose are chilled, the algae blooms among the smooth stones.*
*And wearing away what no one remembers any more*
*is what we do.*

## Leo, Volkssturm conscriptee, drafted from Hitler Youth a week before the end of the war, captured near Jüterbog

And I remember on the second last night we were in the old villa and were standing around in a room on the top storey, and that the tanks' and trucks' vibrations rumbled up through the floor, they were rolling in, and that smoke and fuel smells drifted up from outside, and then another shelling shattered glass over everything and we were thrown into disarray, and Where's the commandant? Edo asked me, and I reminded him that Commandant Lutz had ridden his motorcycle into headquarters to get our orders, that all the wires were down, and we there lay on our stomachs, panting, too shaken to look at each other. And after a few seconds I lifted my head and watched the thick clouds of smoke rising behind the roofs, and then we shut off the lights and dragged ourselves over to the window and I peered over the ledge at the gigantic tanks with the big white stars on them thundering up the street towards us, and the others were looking too, and one of them said, We have to shoot, boys. I shivered, and they looked at me and said, You're not scared are you, Leo? You're not going to pike on us are you, Leo? and I was just cold, but I thought, Oh shit, I must be giving the wrong impression, and I got to my knees and balanced my panzerfaust on the window frame and angled myself at the enemy passing in front of me. I was still confident. Not the filled-to-the-brim confident I'd been the day before, but still confident. I'm part of a military operation, I thought, but doubt had crept into my mind, and it seemed as though we were all pretending that this wasn't actually a nightmare; and then we lined our guns up along the ledge like good little soldiers as some Americans in an armoured truck drove up behind a couple of tanks, shouting for us to surrender, come out. And when one of the goddamn tanks passed right below us and stalled, Edo threw a grenade, which set off a plume of smoke, or steam, but didn't explode, and one of the boys, standing and leaning behind the window frame to get a better angle, shouted for everyone to shoot, and we began firing, but we could see nothing having any effect and Edo said, Shit guys, is this the best we can do? and his friend, Mathias, the star football player from our school, hissed, with his typical guts, You kidding? We'll keep at it till we've got every last one of those pussies, won't we? smiling. So I looked down into the street at the enemy in their trucks and T-34s and aimed at one, and then I pressed the trigger of my panzerfaust, boof, boof, and there was a flaming flash, and simultaneously a scream beside me, and in the shadowy light I saw that Edo had been shot in the face by most of the panzer's explosives blasting out the back instead of down the tube. Less than a minute after that, it was clear that he was burned and dead. And we all began screaming and I shouted at the boys, What do we do now? Where's Commandant Lutz? How're we supposed to know anything? Shit, I followed the rules, I said. And they said, It's written there on the side, Beware! Fire Jet! I said, I know that! Let's quickly move him to the back wall, they said. Yes, I said, and not only because I didn't want to let them see how I was shaking like a leaf. Then one of them dragged him over to the door, and another took off his scarf and wrapped it around Edo's head, and I crawled over and grabbed his tags, because I knew how his mother would want them, and then I could hear feet stomping up the stairs, I could hear the Americans shouting, giving orders, telling each other who knows what, where they thought we were, I suppose, since the town was basically abandoned and anyone who did happen to be there still was in their cellar, and I thought, Shit, this is it, here's where I die and no one will even know what went on, it will always be a mystery. When the two American soldiers burst through the door, they were yelling at us in English. Go home! they shouted. What are you kids even doing in this war? Go home! I remember that while they were shouting they didn't even raise their guns and when the boys went to lift their weapons they snatched everything out of our hands and just made us walk to the truck by shoving us there. And then I said, Are you going to kill us? and one of

them looked at me and smacked me on the side of the head and laughed
and said, We don't shoot children, kiddo.

*They are marching without looking back,*
*marking every stream they pass, every town*
*and river and lake beyond it.*
*Most won't get back home*
*and what remains, the earth will cover. There are plenty*
*of lost strangers in this unpredictable geography,*
*disappearing, never to be found.*
*For there can be no more innocence,*
*no, no more innocence;*
*no more innocence; not again.*

# Second Language

### Ewald
### Hamburg/Melbourne 1979

> We do not meet but in distances
> – Patrick White

Early that morning I wrote, *I'm not really interested in Australia.* That night, looking out at the stars, *On the plane – haven't slept for 36 hours.*

Christmas '78; my father had given me a ticket to visit his sister in Melbourne, and although I was already trying to carve out a name as a travel writer, the kind of travel I had in mind was Turkey, South America, the kind where you didn't have to meet up with people you knew or happened to be related to. I was nineteen, about to move into my first communal house, newly enrolled in the literature course at the University of Hamburg, and spoke only basic English.

In sending me away, he was trying to kill two birds with one stone: the only time he'd gone to Australia he hadn't liked it himself, but he'd promised his mother before she died that he'd keep an eye on my aunt; and he wanted to break up my relationship.

My girlfriend, Luisa Grapl, was twenty-seven, an important member of the SDP and a terrific photographer. She and her family had moved from Bavaria to the north five years earlier when Mr Grapl took on a more lucrative position with the railways. Luisa was nearly twenty-five at that stage, and had recently finished her teaching degree but not yet found a job. It's probably not overstating things to say in those days Luisa basically lived and breathed social activism, and that I was in love with her. She was a regular contributor to political newspapers, journals, going to factories, meetings, demonstrations, writing articles, but it was in her photographs she was her most convincing. I think it was because her pictures conveyed an ordinary humanness, no matter how dramatic the circumstances. When I met her, she was living in an old storehouse building at Netteinburg, right next to the station. The conditions were terrible. She was often hungry. The drainage systems in the area were so old, she said, that once a pre-war jar of gherkins floated up from the sewer. That first night we slept at the abandoned shop she shared with friends (massive whitewashed windows, damp walls) on her mattress on the floor. And what will you tell this fierce father of yours tomorrow? she said to me. Nothing, I said, and kissed the lids of her dark eyes.

Three months later, I joined the party too. That year, 1976, more demonstrations were in West Germany than ever before. There were heavy black clouds casting shadows over the entire country, and although Baader and Meinhof and the whole red militant guerrilla catastrophe were often lumped together with every form of social activism going, I certainly didn't believe in shooting anyone or blowing people up. But when I tried talking about these things with my parents, it soon became clear there was no point. With no patience for Luisa or her 'ideology', they wouldn't speak to her or even let her in the house. My father said Luisa must have problems, why else would she be with a boy? I can't remember them having a conversation that went for more than a minute so on what basis he formed his opinions I can't say. I know he thought I was ruining my life.

On the morning I was to leave Hamburg, I said goodbye to my mother and brother and phoned Luisa, and my father drove me to Frankfurt, through Hanover and Göttingen and Kassel, and I don't think we spoke a word to each other except to argue about how far up or down the car window should go. I was depressed, found it hard to eat anything. And the flight went on for days.

Finally I made it to Australia and my aunt's house in Heidelberg (!) where I switched to lighter clothes (though nothing felt light enough) and met my cousins: at the time, Aunt S still had all seven of her children living at home. But the heat was unbearable, and to get away from it I had to go the bathroom, lie on the cool tiles while my aunt – a bulky, handsome woman with striking pale blue eyes and who only ever wore dresses or skirts, never pants, and had it in her head that wherever I went she should go with me – would traipse upstairs and call to me through the door.

Each night she'd lay out plans for the following day: taking me on trams to public gardens, the city, Captain Cook's Cottage; in her car along narrow roads to tourist spots in the surrounding hills, or on tours of wineries, pointing out on the way places of personal interest, where she'd had her first ice cream in Australia, the stretches that had been fields when they'd arrived and were now taken up with highways and houses and service stations, where she'd bought a nice scarf, or a tub of honey made from the nectar of a particular eucalypt blossom, and we'd find somewhere to stop for coffee, which was always accompanied by a cake of some sort, and she'd keep talking about the holidays she wanted to take and music, Strauss, Bruckner, Puccini, the state of the Catholic Church, how little her children appreciated opera, the sacrifices she and her husband had had to make, my uncle's heart condition, everything really, everything that preoccupied and bothered her. Yet despite this, I liked hearing her talk. Somehow her complaints didn't sound like complaining. And sooner or later we'd get back in the car and drive to the next designated stop, and I'd watch the bush slip by into the distance, my eyelids fluttering – I always got so sleepy, it was hazy and warm, the sun shining in the treetops – and I thought it was beautiful. Once we were back at the house, Aunt S would then head to the kitchen to make dinner, while I sat in the living room, reading through the books on Australia my uncle had lent me or drifting into memories of being with Luisa.

The thing was, although my older cousins had spoken German when they were little, they'd forgotten most of it once they went to school, claiming they'd been teased, and they barely talked to me. Perhaps it was my English, but we were separated as if by glass. Sometimes they disappeared into the surrounding rooms and I could hear their laughter; perhaps they were laughing at the way I'd pronounced something, perhaps it was my glasses, perhaps it was my name, or what I wore, perhaps whatever it was they found so entertaining had nothing to do with me. In any case, they left me largely to my own devices and I mostly hung out with my aunt and uncle, a doctor who, though Australian, had lived in Europe for twenty years and spoke fluent German, because I didn't know what else to do.

\*

One night, almost halfway through my six-week stay, my aunt suggested we take a trip. What about the Little Desert? she said. I'd been looking at brochures the day before and mentioned to her that I was curious to see what lay further afield, away from the coast where, I'd read, most of the population lived.

So the following morning we headed out of the city and drove through country that flowed through your eyes like a wasteland. It made the hairs stand up on my arms. It was not desert as such, not for most of the way, but the landscape was wide, barren, the kind that brings a dazed nervousness to the way you think. I thought about the atomic bombs that had been tested not so far off, not so long ago. I thought about the snakes and spiders and dingoes. When my aunt pulled up to the motel, five hours after we'd left the outskirts of suburban Melbourne, she said, Do you want to swim before nightfall? I thought about the scorpions and mosquitoes. If it's okay, I said, no, I won't.

The next day, the sun rolled from the horizon, hard and white. The window to our room was long and faced east, and the pool, shiny in the dawn light, lay spread out in front, flat as a stone. A concrete wall sliced the view to the national park and over the stunted trees hung a huge oblong of blue sky. Seen from this angle, the highway was a featureless strip of bitumen tapering to nowhere; its stillness looked like fake stillness, like the staging of stillness.

By 7.30 a.m., we were standing outside under the clacking fronds of half a palm, waiting for the tour bus to pick us up, and when it arrived it was already close to full, with the group looking calmly out at us from their seats as if we weren't part of reality. At first, Aunt S just sat taking a lot of pictures with her heavy big camera. I was on the aisle. She said she would make copies of the photos for me so that I would have mementoes of the adventure. She seemed very happy. Then she went back to talking about everything, especially how I couldn't really know what it was like to live under the Communists and how quickly things can change, and then we both fell silent, watching the scenery moving by through the bus window.

Later that afternoon, after having visited several points of interest, and eating lunch by a waterhole, we turned and headed back towards the town and our motel. There was a little daylight still, the sandy scrubland breaking into a stippled yellowish ocean. The insects were rising in clouds into the air.

Walking through the bush earlier, I'd thought, predictably, of Luisa, would we stay together and travel like this? In my bag was a postcard, which I'd got two days before from my friend Thomas, a fellow social democrat and party organiser, asking me whether distance had provided me with any new or insightful ideas on helping the proletariat and what I thought I might write about next. Generally, there were six to ten of us at any one time working on the magazine. Thomas ran things as he seemed to have no trouble staying up all night. He was divorced, and in a relationship with an older man connected to the publishing side of operations. In a vague sort of way, they looked like each other. They used the same gestures, and dressed in similar cotton shirts and dark jeans. Both wore their hair with a thick fringe to one side. The other contributors were of varying ages and backgrounds; Oskar and Carol were students majoring in law, Otto and Paul were working in factories, and Ulric was unemployed. And naturally there was Luisa too, who took her role as visual documenter very seriously. The rest were a floating circle, involved when they felt passionately about something, or were bored.

I had written in a letter back to him that same night. I said I wasn't sure, that I'd got the impression that the struggle for civil and political rights had become slightly out of control and I'd begun to think I possibly didn't have the courage necessary to pursue things along those lines. Privately, I imagined putting together long, comprehensive pieces dealing with youth and activism across the world, as well as distributing pamphlets, gathering material, so that I didn't feel so unconvinced by what I was doing with my life. At the same time, I imagined Luisa and me renting an apartment on Rosenstrasse and walls lined with her most famous photographs, perhaps even a baby, though up to that point there'd been no indication from her that she was interested in anything like that. I remembered a time several months before, sitting with her and some friends in a bar on the bank of the Außenalster lake; it was during the first weeks of our getting together and I'd asked her to tell us about herself. She said she couldn't think what I might want to know, but that she liked working and she liked art, and that she didn't have much money, which we could have guessed, and that she wanted to be happy and good at something just like everybody else. Thomas said she thought she also liked conspiracy and she looked embarrassed. He asked how many men she had been with. She leant over, put her hand on his knee, said not as many as he had.

The understanding that seemed to exist between them made me uncomfortable: too often, Thomas seemed to be laughing over nothing. Then Luisa told us about her brother Stefan, his job as a runner on movie sets in Los Angeles, and a girlfriend, Alys, that Stef had had while still at school. Luisa said what happened to Alys had somehow deepened her involvement with left-wing politics, even though she'd always found her hard to take (evidently she made stupid jokes about Hanns-Marten Schleyer and the Lufthansa hijacking, that sort of thing).

Everything turned for Luisa when, one day, Alys had come over to the Grapls' place for lunch, eventually revealing that her father had kicked her out of the house and she had nowhere else to go. Later that afternoon, after Mrs Grapl had tried calling Alys's parents a number of times, she finally agreed to let Stef and Luisa walk her home to check the lie of the land. Mrs Grapl said she was sure everything would blow over, that Alys's father was just worried, and how it was normal for him to have trouble adjusting to the fact that his daughter was not a little girl any more. Mr Grapl said if need be she could spend the night with them.

On the way there, Luisa noticed that Alys became more and more agitated, prattling away non-stop, acting excited all of a sudden. She gave a vehement speech on the importance of the Italian Masters and told them she owned two genuine Tintoretto woodcuts. Luisa didn't know if she really owned the pictures or was just bragging, and while she listened to her, hearing her yabbering on, the high sing-songy whine of her voice getting to her more and more, she had the impression that Alys was, in fact, helplessly naive. Her talk seemed artificial, childish, and she kept repeating to herself, 'You know I don't want to live here any more,' over and over, like a scratched record.

When they reached her street, huddled at the front of the apartment block were her parents, a few neighbours and a couple of police officers – her mother, who owned the most popular sporting goods store in the area, Luisa said, resting one foot, toes down, behind her, as if she were a horse in the shade on a warm afternoon. Alys's father was very short. Luisa saw one of the male police officers move towards Alys in a way that meant she wasn't to go anywhere, hand on her shoulder, and Alys somehow holding herself differently, now unexpectedly mute and compliant, like she was waiting for a bus. Then her father came over to Luisa and Stef and, having thanked them, said this was a personal situation and told them to leave.

At school the next day, the headmistress called Stef and Luisa in and asked them to tell her what they knew about Alys before the crime squad arrived to make investigations regarding the two girls in Alys's hockey team who'd got sick the day before and nearly died; hospital tests revealed toxic levels of arsenic in their bloodstreams. After Alys chose to come straight out and tell them how she'd put weedkiller in their (free school) milk and was given a three-year sentence in a youth state detention centre, Stef never saw her again, though the Grapls marked the slide into what they called his 'delinquency' from this point, and he spent the next couple of years moving between institutions and her grandmother's house, where he sat for hours on the porch drinking and listening to punk music and smoking grass. For Luisa, both Stef's and Alys's behaviour was the direct result of their lives of petit bourgeois repression. This, she told us, had inspired her to sign up with the party.

The story was not an unfamiliar one for those there with us at the bar, I think. Some minutes went by, then a bunch of them moved to the dance floor and one of them, Marta, grabbed my elbow, dragged me right to the middle of the crowd, giving me a particularly glorious smile. I remember the song playing was 'Fox on the Run', and the floor was a kind of fake parquet and sticky. I remember I could feel her fingers pressing hard into my arm. She said, So who are the writers you like best? loudly, but I realised whoever I said she would most likely disagree, as I knew she did with most things, and I shrugged. Over her shoulder I watched Luisa hugging someone goodbye. Here, come closer, Marta said, raising her arms towards the ceiling and shaking them a couple of times to slide the bangles down from her wrists. I pretended I hadn't heard. Come closer, she shouted again, and hooking me round the waist pulled me towards her, her bangles digging into my back. She said, I can see how you're her type, she seems to have a special fondness for middle-class guys with literary pretensions, and she kissed me on the cheek. Her eyes looked strange to me, glassy, as if she'd done too many drugs. I laughed. She did too. Then I twisted myself free, made my way back to Luisa at the bar, and Marta turned to her friends again, went on dancing.

*

The wonder of God's universe, Aunt S said to me, eating biscuits from the complimentary packets she'd taken from the motel, crumbs slipping from her mouth into the gullies of her skirt, as the bus made its way back to town. We slipped past a world gritty and quivering, like a shucked mussel, open and full of small ridges and curves. It's how I imagine *The Sheltering Sky*, I said, but she didn't answer.

And so I gazed ahead to where the windscreen offered a rectangular piece of view, framing a world that flickered from light to dark as erratically as a film. A little way along, congregated in a sprawling mass across the road, was a herd of kangaroos, big as cows, scattered as casually as a handful of coins.

My aunt reached out and began excitedly thumping my leg. Look, she said, and I nodded, but then as we drove close to the indolent-seeming animals, we suddenly began to skid.

There was a jolt and a tremendous thud, and Aunt S jerked and tipped into my lap, while over her shoulder, out the window, I saw several kangaroos flying through the air in an arc the length of the vehicle, then tumble to the ground.

The bus slid to a halt. We all filed out. Glancing about, I saw that one corner of the vehicle was completely caved in, as though squeezed by a giant thumb, the headlights were smashed, the mirror swung from the side like the broken antennae on a moth, shards of shattered mirror were sprinkled over the gravel…and flung in every direction around us were the dead or dying kangaroos, the rest having fled into the tangled, low scrub.

It should be put out of pain, said Aunt S next to me, gazing over at a big kangaroo still half wedged under a front wheel by its tail.

Inside the bus, I could see the driver speaking into a long distance radio, reporting what had happened back to base.

I said I didn't think there was anyone there who could do anything.

There are men here, she said, as nearby, the animal hardly breathing, twitched aimlessly, as if swimming against the tide, flailing, then momentarily resigned, before clawing again uselessly at the air.

I asked if perhaps the driver kept a gun, driving as he did on these long deserted roads.

But, Only farmers have guns, said Aunt S. And she sighed, patted my arm, and walked behind the coach and vanished from sight, returning a moment later with a man not much older than I was.

She showed him the kangaroo and he stared at it with the expression children use for unfamiliar food, depressed and bashful. He hooked two fingers around the neck of his T-shirt, not saying anything, then turned and climbed back into the bus. Re-emerging not long after, we saw that cradled in his arms he had his guitar in its hard case (he'd strummed song requests for everyone earlier over the campfire lunch). He was sweating. He wiped a cheek on one shoulder, thrust out his chin, shifted his legs apart a little and, raising his guitar case, brought it down on the kangaroo. It made a feeble, barely perceptible sound as it rolled to the side, and we saw a dead joey, still virtually embryonic, slither noiselessly from its pouch onto the dust.

How sad, but that's everything taken care of, said my aunt.

And we got back into the bus with the rest of the passengers and continued slowly along the highway.

The sun was nearly below the skyline. The lights of the distant shops and houses wavering in the falling darkness looked like tiny fishing boats on the water at night – there was no moon yet – and I breathed that strange, metal smell of the desert at sunset as it streamed in through the open windows.

Nearing the motel, my aunt opened the case to her camera hoping to take more photos, but the lens was bent and wouldn't screw on properly, so she put the camera into her bag, leaned her forehead on the glass pane of the window, and instead of looking through the viewfinder as she'd done for so much of the day, she cupped her hands around her face and stared out like she was staring through a sort of telescope. It was so dark, the contours of the bush swallowed by the night sky, I couldn't imagine what she was looking at.

But then she said, Here, look, and told me to swap seats and peering out I saw how the air was filled with beetles, shooting up, skimming around one another. They were not exactly beautiful but they had a mad, driven, delicate energy that for some reason stirred up in me clumsy mixed feelings of wonder and pain, reminded me, for some reason, of the last days I'd spent with Luisa, by the lake, and I began crying like a baby.

Aunt S took my hand, told me I'd be home soon, that she could see how tired I was and that later we'd have a long beer in the motel bar, to relax.

\*

The next day, we made our way back to Melbourne, stopping for lunch at a café attached to a service station that had the wreckage of cars piled up next to the toilet block, and then we continued until we reached the house, where my all my cousins were either out or hiding in their rooms, and I went and lay down on my bed, and tried to sleep for half an hour before dinner but couldn't. Maybe it was because of being *over*tired, which sometimes happens when I've had the kind of night I'd had the night before; I'd slept badly, with half remembered dreams which affected me even after I was awake. In one, I recall, Luisa was trying to drown a child in snowshoes and loose jumper in the Außenalster, her face turned away from the little boy, because of the splashing. It must sound like I was angry with her, or frightened, but I wasn't; whatever it was, it was probably more to do with my uncertainty about everything.

And that night, when we collected for dinner, my uncle handed me a letter from my father. I put it in my pocket, went up to the bathroom and lay down on the tiles – I couldn't bring myself to open it – until I heard the footsteps on the stairs, and knocking, and then my aunt's face appeared at the door, and she looked at me kindly and asked if everything was all right.

It's okay, nothing's wrong, I said. It's hot, I'm just washing my face, and surprisingly, once I had, I felt better.

When she sat beside me on the edge of the bath and reached for my hand, I wanted to say, Throw this letter into the bin on your way out, can you? but it would have shocked her, and she in fact smiled and said, He's only saying what he believes is right, and Of course, I said, because I had three weeks to go, and I was counting them down and she knew it.

Then she walked towards the doorway and, brightening her voice, told me that tomorrow we would drive to the Great Ocean Road, which is where we'd see the Twelve Apostles. Before dinner, my uncle had been showing me some brochures with pictures of the curious rock formations rising up from the sea.

For a long while, I sat on the rim of the bath – I knew everyone else was at the table eating, even though there was almost no sound coming from the dining room, and I wanted to get up and join them, but I couldn't seem to move. I shut my eyes. I perched with my body hunched, listening to the neighbours through the open window, jumping into their pool, their splashing, choppy paddling, the excessive laughter that kids always make when they're clowning around, and as the minutes passed I thought my aunt would reappear but no one came, and so I sat there – heard my breathing under the noise of the world outside – and then I rinsed my face again and went downstairs.

# What Name Will You See When You Do Not Hear a Sound?

### Klara Schmidt (née Leonhardt)
### Chemnitz, 1929

> I know who I am and who I may be, if I choose.
> – Cervantes

Compliance is a stone wall,
but you can climb it.
Helene Leonhardt, twenty-seven years old,

grew up my niece
and now she is my daughter.
It is May. Today

in the garden, I saw her arm
reach out to him
like the neck of a bridal swan:

him, with his possibility of kindness,
of mending wounds; where hope
has a chance of taking hold.

I watched him kiss her. And her little smile
of something indefinable:
she is a difficult woman.

I wanted to tell them, Look,
Deuteronomy is mad – *A man*
*of illegitimate birth*

*shall not enter the congregation of the Lord* –
but I don't know.
You can see how what's written

raises inevitable silences. Standing
under the birches
the two of them talked, the pond

bits of glass in the trees gaps,
the wind arranging the grass briskly
from a dark blue sky, until

night closed in. Clouds
pocketed the stars. I was
propping tomorrow's bundle for the post office

on the hallstand by the door when they finally
came in. On the bottom of each
invitation she's put Helene Schmidt.

It is the language of consent.

# Rope in the Snow

## S and C
## Güstrow: the GDR, December 1951

At the edge of the forest — dream flowers tinkle, flash, flare —
— Rimbaud

No matter how late it gets, C isn't going to sleep. His sister, S, is near the window, curled up, tranquil. She has braided honey-coloured hair coiled like two sleek molluscs.

When he sees she's about to doze, he scrapes a lump of sludge from one shoe with the toe of the other and flicks it in her direction, asks — House or garden? What do you miss the most?

She frowns. — It's too long ago, she says.

— Remember the picture in the hall, the picture of the island with the black trees?

— I don't know. I think so.

He reaches to prod her. She pulls away and turns her back to him.

They are sitting at a table with their mother in the waiting room at the station in Güstrow, and C is determined to stay awake because in the past few hours he's noticed their neighbour W, who has chosen to leave for the West too, moving his chair closer to their mother, moving his chair to make it look like he's letting others in or stretching his crooked, rigid leg that's missing a foot, and slyly squeezing his shoulder up against hers.

C leans towards S. — You know, a man in a white sheet, being rowed across the sea?

— Isle of the Dead, says W, in a voice loud enough for everyone to hear.

He is a small man with yellow teeth and one of those thin little moustaches that have become popular in these parts since the start of the fifties.

After having stood around for so long, most people there have stopped talking and are now reading or napping: every so often, someone will push open the door, hoping to see the train approach in the cold darkness outside; the night remains blank and impenetrable.

– You know the one I mean, Pupee? C says, ignoring W as he does with those he doesn't like and in the way that so often embarrasses his mother. – The dark clouds and sea, and that spooky figure in the moonlight?'

S sits there, not saying anything. She doesn't want to be drawn in; she remembers the painting as an indissoluble hole into which the light disappeared. At moments she invents memories – thin cotton dresses, apple trees bent with fruit in the orchard behind their house in Deutsch Krone (as it was known then – it's Walcz now) her grandmother's hands, her grandmother's nail scissors, huge metal pots steaming with red cabbage – or at least they feel invented now, when she thinks of them, the absences looking back at her such that she's constantly having to tell herself they were things she probably dreamed. Yet the painting she remembers with not just her mind, but her body: a thin, radiating unease that ran through her bones to the marrow whenever she'd passed it on the way to her mother's bedroom.

C continues to nudge her. – The cliffs were steep and there was no one else on the ocean. No one on the island. Remember?

S buries her face deep into the crook of an elbow, like a jackal settling into a grass hollow. – I don't know, she says. All I really remember is getting our morning sweet from Oma, and I'm tired, don't you understand?

\*

Beside them, L is looking through the papers she has for her family and the tickets to Lübeck. The first time she'd heard there was to be an amnesty for border crossings on Stalin's birthday she'd assumed it was wishful thinking. She ignored it as she did most rumours until her son, C, began to talk about the Forst's and the Becker's and other families in the neighbourhood who were packing to go. C is seventeen and justifiably focused on his future, which includes study at Berlin or Mannheim university and, from there, Oxford: a Shakespeare devotee, someone he's read mostly in translation, C has fantasies of living in England and immersing himself in English literature.

But L who is, generally speaking, indecisive, has been as uncertain in the matter of whether they should stay or go as she is with anything. Only after a series of dreams – a desolate village junction, a man with burning eyes waving a sabre – which she's interpreted as omens, has she been able to get what little money and things she has together and inform her children that they will, in fact, be moving again.

\*

Seven hours later, at 2 a.m., she is beginning to think they should probably head back to the house: then she hears the train grinding along the tracks and, squeezing her daughter's arm tightly, stands up. – Do you need to go to the toilet?

– The toilet?

– It will probably be better here than in there.

For a moment, L fantasises again that there is a state you can get to where tasks like this can be abandoned, were no longer necessary, a privilege which for some reason as a child she'd imagined was among those enjoyed by royalty.

\*

Once they've realised the train is approaching, the guards walk over and block the exit. Whenever a chair is pushed back, or a door slammed, Stalin's picture rattles on the wall.

\*

C sees his mother, a slight woman with narrow shoulders, stumble slightly and he steps across to offer a hand. He takes her case as well as his own. When he looks for his sister, he sees she's already by the door, waiting with a group of school friends. They are all close in age, thirteen or fourteen, a uniform bunch in brown woollen coats, scarves and leather boots.

C is the eldest, a tall boy with glossy black hair that hangs like an axe over his forehead. He has a certain way of regarding people through his glasses, almost as if he's deaf, strangely removed, and even when he's speaking there's a sense of distance, a way of talking as if he's worried he won't be understood, a tone of separation that carries with it a muted yet vague sense of threat. He hears what people are saying not as sentences but as coded messages. It is the condition of a body that has no assumptions left in it. Or, at least, a body that calculates what method, what intent, is at work behind whatever is said.

But – Are you all right? C asks W, adopting a concerned note while helping him with his crutches.

Of course, C respects W, although he has nowhere near the amount of respect the women have for him. As it is, this is the last day W will spend in the town where he grew up: thirty years from now, as an eighty-one-year-old dying in an alms house in Husum, he will shrug to the nurse caring for him, 'Damn those Bolsheviks. But I probably did better than I deserved.'

Lately, C has tried imagining what it was like for the prisoners in the concentration camps – the kind which had held his father along with W. He remembers W telling him, after he got back from Leningrad in 1947, 'Prison chooses its survivors.' A stupid fatalistic statement yet, when pressed for more, what comes out is barely useful. 'I'm afraid these days my memory lets me down,' he'll say to C. 'I know your father remained honourable. He wasn't very strong, though, and there wasn't much in the area of modern medicine that the Soviet doctors were capable of.' Then how did you make it back? thinks C. I bet he shot himself, he thinks.

He feels a rush of nausea from the torment of longing and sleepless rage. He follows his mother and W over to where his sister and her companions stand talking in tired humdrum voices. Their eyes are darting from left to right the whole time as they speak, their heads tucked into their shoulders; a habit developed from years of not trusting who might be trying to listen to their conversations. The room is filled with the heavy mournful smell of wet flannel. After tonight, I hope I never have to smell this smell again, thinks C, sticking his nose into cupped hands. But what 'never' means at this point in his life he doesn't know.

– Isle of the Dead, yes, W says with a deep gurgling chuckle – Every house in Prussia must have had that picture on its walls.

\*

When S was three, the Luftwaffe Jüterbog Division approved Chief Technical Engineer HH's request for leave to visit his family in Deutsch Krone. He was a man of average height and average nationalist loyalties, summoned in 1939 from his successful manufacturing business to contribute to the cause of the Third Reich. H loved his boy, but he especially saw his daughter as pure relief, the essence of innocence and unnecessary beauty. Sometimes he would take her down to the Buchwald café, south past the cemetery where his own father was buried, through the forest and along the lake, talking, S riding on his shoulders, and on this particular day he walked telling her stories of Big Hermel and the Knight of Stauffenberg, which she didn't understand naturally, but she knew – gauging from the expansion in his chest or the lilt of his voice – when to laugh, or be silent. The ice on the lake had melted, blobs of sunlight were splotched across the dense leaf-mulched earth, new sprung fungi the colour and texture of hard-boiled eggs clung to the roots of the beeches and elms. H felt the strength in his back, and the contrasting softness of his daughter's small thighs, chest, fingers. She was fair-haired and smiling. Her eyes were like two cut gems.

Along the way, he remembered walking with L down these paths, in the weeks before they were married. Everything he'd hoped to relieve her of now seemed to be re-entering her world: the incredible loneliness, the arbitrary domestic arrangements. He had to smother the unease the name Hitler stirred in him. In their seven years together before the start of the war, L's ravaged spirit had seemed infinitely lighter. Truthfully, he knew there were certain facts of his wife's past he was still to learn. But he also had it in his head that her air of sadness was essentially from some primal sense, developed as an orphan when she'd been sent to various institutions and foster homes and suffered terrible abuse, that she was once again being targeted.

As they got to the café, H glanced at the people sitting around tables on the terrace and chose a spot near the corner in a bathtub-shaped piece of shade, where he could keep his eye on his small daughter, an energetic girl who might try to join the other kids racing round the surrounding trees and be knocked over. He went inside and ordered a coffee. Then he opened a window, leant out and asked if she'd like a pretzel. S gave a joyous shriek of laughter and waved. H picked up a *Berliner Illustrirte Zeitung* and went outside and sat down again and flipped through the paper waiting for his order to be brought out to him. He sat and read till an elderly neighbour, a big woman with a red face, called from the other side of the terrace, Wasn't that his little girl down there? Who was watching her? Did he know she'd wandered onto the jetty, taken off her shoes, and slipped, falling into the water?

He immediately sprang to his feet and ran as fast as he could to the end of the dock. He saw a clump of people, leaning over the dock's edge, reaching down into the still lake. Under the water, the girl flailed and paddled with her two podgy arms, face up, looking up at him with wide blue eyes, her mouth open, thrashing her little body about with great insistence, and after wondering momentarily at how so much force below failed to stir the surface, how there was no disturbance, not the slightest ripple visible, H threw his jacket onto the boards of the jetty and jumped in. It wasn't deep and, like a trout hauled into the sun, S jerked and smacked her pale fleshy limbs against him, sucking air into her lungs, until finally growing limp with soundless tiredness she nuzzled in and lapsed sleepily on his shoulder.

Relief swam through his bones. With his daughter still half asleep in his arms, before setting off for home, he bought her another pretzel, as well as an almond cake, and she was incredibly happy. H thought his wife was probably right and that S was going to get on well in life, because life these days required a clarity of will and resilience, which, along with an unquestioning nature and simple sensuous desires, and the care and guidance of her parents, S clearly possessed; possibly it would be good, he thought, if he were to adopt something of her vigorous *joie de vivre* nature, not in a naive way that was a secret denial of the struggles of existence, but as a function of human resourcefulness.

Back home that night, he gathered his belongings and packed for the return journey to the airfield near Berlin. As usual, the nanny took care of S and her brother while H and L ate a formal dinner with the extended family at the long table in the dining room; the mantels were lined with vases of flowers. His clothes were washed and drying in the attic where the housekeeper had hung them. When he left at dawn, he didn't remember his shoes, which were airing outside on the coal bin. Once she'd seen them, the day after he'd gone, L didn't want them moved. S noticed them there, still wrinkled and only slightly faded, when they clambered into the truck, freezing and terrified, fleeing from the advancing Russian forces five years later.

*

On the far end of the station platform, W talks about Dürer and Caspar David Friedrich, he talks about Marlene Dietrich and Gitte Alpar, he asks L whether she's seen the films of Fritz Lang. He tells her he's seen *M* seven times and *Der goldene See* is on his list of the top ten films of all time. – Makes me want to go to America! he says to L. – From here on in, let's turn our eyes to America!

C wants to convince his mother she owes W nothing, but she has been reared not to question. She nods, inspecting her cuffs with all her might.

– In America, W says, history is permanently triumphant.

– You think? C says.

– And because Prussia no longer exists, this side of the world is now blighted –

– There are murderers in America too, you know, C cuts in.

– War is murder, we all know that. No decent man wants to kill anyone!

A woman, who has sat across from the prattling W for four hours without saying a word, now hisses a curse from out the corner of her mouth – Brought up on pig's blood the lot of them, she says, which makes everyone laugh out loud.

– It's something you learn, W goes on, doing his best to keep the mood of the conversation light so that the boy would stay onside with him.

The doors to the train remain barred. No way for C to get away.

– Well, that's how it was for me, he says. I was forty-two, rather old for the Wehrmacht. I was employed at a spring factory, but my hands had slowed. I was on the way out. But then there came the military. The military saw to it that I was spruced up and of use again! And who can tell? Maybe Prussia will be returned to us one day. Maybe. Maybe. Until then, he says, his voice plunging to a conspiratorial whisper, let's concentrate on getting out from under these communists. Then perhaps we can make it to America.

Everything W says to C is completely annoying to him.

\*

They were near the back of the crowd when the train doors are finally opened. Calls from the guards: *Alle ordentlich zu bleiben!* Everyone boarding is to remain orderly. They were used to commands, but what does order mean when your carriage is a cattle wagon? Perhaps, C said to himself, order can just be wilful blindness, blindness like hide-and-seek, blindness like a game.

W gripped his crutches tight and said, or rather urged L hoarsely from behind – Push, my dear woman.

\*

It is C, however, holding their cases aloft, thrusting them this way and that, who forges a path through. Eleven boxcars line the platform – to be pulled by an SŽD Eel2 locomotive, he notices: nothing like the trains that for those summers during the early 40s took them to Schwerin: look what they must travel in now, them, the well-to-do Hs, with their industrial piping cartel, three-storey house on Konigstrasse, elegant red geranium-decked balconies, fully fitted electric lighting (first in town) and private motor vehicles (also first in town) and a wonderful endless rambling garden which smelled of sand and earth and plums and sun and which C desires to smell so strongly again his throat hurts.

– Watch Mutti, he says to S.

To which she thinks, tipping under the weight of her own bag, What could I do if anything were to happen? And anyway, their mother is actually more *there* for once for goodness sake.

– You realise we can never come back, he says.

– You don't know.

– Of course we can't.

– Would you want to?

– Who knows?

– I know.

– No you don't, you don't know anything, he says, relishing the authority he believes himself to have and kissing her on the head.

When they get to the front, they scramble aboard, C helping his sister, then one of her friends and her mother, then W into the cattle car.

L stands there paralysed until they begin dragging her up by her coat sleeves.

*

They had the night, a day, another night of cold sunless December to get through, and L was conscious of the distance disappearing away under them because as they clattered along the silverish tracks, never ending, frozen silverish tracks that trailed them into the black featureless landscape she could see the rails through the gaps in the wooden floor, and the endless rails, and sleepers, ice crusted on bolts and in grooves.

*

We must be in God's favour, C reflected, settling with his copies of *Sonette* and *Gebetbuch* into a corner. He fell into a kind of prayer that kept rhythm with the sounds of the train, repeating over in his mind, *Pater Noster, Pater Noster*; the only aspect of his desired conversion to Catholicism his mother found hard to take was the language…

S was almost asleep again. Although she will forget almost everything from these years after marrying and moving to Australia, she'll remember this journey her whole life; in 1969, when restitution for properties in Berlin is introduced, she'll buy a brand-new Rover 2000 with what she inherits the from the sale of her paternal grandmother's apartment block in Charlottenburg, finally getting her driver's licence at thirty-five, and she'll find herself thinking of this trip, of what they went through to get out, even as one or other of her own children asks her about her experiences during the war and what she 'knew' and she will always tell them – Nothing – what could we know? All we could think about was survival.

*

L continued peering at the light flickering through the slats until W lit a cigarette. She lifted her face with a half-stunned, half-dazed look and then, bored by his talk about movies and art, once again turned her back to him – W, apparently the last man known to have seen her husband, the companionable bulk of her husband H, who, as she'd heard from some of the returned soldiers, instead of having died in that camp hospital in Leningrad might have simply been moved to work among the other living corpses elsewhere on the roads or in the pits, like Siberia.

*

W's hand appeared on her leg.

– Don't worry… It will be all right. Do you hear me? It will be all right…

L snapped her legs back and slid them beneath her. She was irritated by the cigarette smoke, groping about in her pockets for a handkerchief, when a woman called across the compartment – Frau H?

L looked over.

– It's Frau T, the woman said. The shopkeeper – remember me? From Gleviner Strasse?

L smiled weakly.

– How are you, C? Frau T asked, looking across at him and he nodded uneasily: *Pater noster qui es in caelis*. Our father in heaven. Our fathers in heaven.

S woke and slowly stretched her arms to the ceiling. – I'm hungry.

C drew an apple from his pocket; it sat in his palm like a rusted grenade. Then he twisted it till it split in two and handed her half. – Don't eat too fast, Pupee. You don't want another stomach ache.

Next to Frau T, scrutinising him but saying nothing, were her children. C took out a second apple and passed it to them.

– Oh, thank you, said Frau T. Isn't that nice?

The children, clumped together like rags gazed at him, tired and despondent. Then they lay down, spread themselves across their mother's lap and took turns on the apple, chewing drowsily.

*

S swallowed the last of hers, watching from where she sat huddled on the floor opposite. During their trip across the defeated landscape, between naps, she often sang, in her head, songs she'd learned at school, in the choir, or tunes Greta – their nanny back home – had sung to her. The songs were Christmas carols and folk melodies. *In Stille Nacht*. Why did this little song spring to mind all the time? Simply because Brahms had been Greta's favourite – her absolute favourite – of all the composers? And yet, sometimes she heard her mother singing it too…

When S thought back, something that already she didn't like to find herself doing, it was as if she had never really been there, home. If she was shown photos and told, 'This is a picture of the old wagon on the estate, and this is you and your cousin playing by the well, and this was taken on the lake where we liked to swim,' the gap in what she saw and what she felt made them seem like fantastic visions. Instead, she focused her energies on what she understood of the present and the needs of a body that had started bulging like a seed pod, made constant demands, was always plagued by pangs of cold and hunger, and bled on itself.

\*

They are stretched beside one another in the dark. The cattle car they are riding in has been equipped with straw mattresses and a stove. The toilet is a hole sawn in the floor. The whole carriage is able watch if you have to use it. People huddle where they can, talking quietly, sharing sandwiches with wurst, and cigarettes and liquor, and regarding each other with brief stealthy glances.

It is very cold. C is reading his book on pre-industrial engineering, but he's uncomfortable because the silverware in S's bag that he has lodged under his legs is digging into his calves. The catastrophe that was the war has left them with just an envelope of photos and this silver cutlery set, engraved with an unknown person's initials, FWL. The silverware had belonged to a Dresden relative of his mother's for fifty years or more before she'd gone to live in Chemnitz.

What they had once they will never get back. C supposes this is what God has intended, and he thinks, Nothing is about this world. *Sanctificetur nomen tuum*: everything in His name. This thought has been clearly imprinted in his mind for as long as he can remember, it has underpinned everything he has said and done, becoming ever more deeply impressed with the passing of time. And it will underscore any decision he makes for the rest of his life, undeterred by the effects it may have on those he loves, as it predictably will do on the two sons he will have after completing his degree in Cambridge, returning to Germany to teach English and history and marrying K, a girl he'd known in Deutsch Krone, attributing their reacquaintance, not surprisingly, to divine providence. For almost ten years, he'll not be on speaking terms with either of his children, who will reject all Western religions, and spend most of their twenties living in a series of communes in Hamburg: when his first grandchild is born, he will refuse to see him because his parents are unmarried.

\*

Along with the apples, C has a pack of sweets he shares around. The hours have dragged on, and by the time he feels he won't be able to fend off sleep much longer dawn is visible through the cracks in the paling walls.

Almost everyone is asleep alongside him. Twice during the night he's looked up from his book and seen his mother wriggling out of W's reach. The next time, it is Frau T's thigh W is resting his hand on; she is sleeping on his shoulder, oblivious. His persistence appals yet fascinates C; he thinks about human will, then he thinks about redemption, *Adveniat regnum tuum, fiat voluntas tua…*

\*

Meanwhile, with Frau T's unknowing head slipping off in the other direction, W reaches his right arm across and unhooks the latch to the stove door with the end of his crutch, poking at the embers inside to little effect.

A faded orange light seeps over their feet and legs and works its way up to their faces. *Panem nostrum quotidianum da nobis hodie*: C supposes daily needs are open to interpretation, are about proportion, making what you can out of what you have.

L, sensing movement, opens her eyes. Her cheeks are pale as stone. Her hands, like the muzzles of dogs, burrow into the coat sleeves. She watches W stoke the tinder in the stove till it flares. He leans back, the warmth from the fire gradually creeping up the length of their bodies, leaving the stove door open. L remains motionless for a long time, dazzled by the fire, impassive, dreaming.

W sits flushed, with outstretched arms and flattened palms. – I am sorry for you, he says.

She looks at him and says nothing.

– God knows, I wish I could help you.

Silence.

– I am at your service… Do you know what I mean?

L looks away.

At that moment, sparks that have been smouldering on the tip of W's crutch drop to the hessian cover of the straw mattress and catch alight. L shrinks back, but makes no sound.

– Hey, Onkel, watch what you're doing! C's face is distorted and tense. His voice is tight, it is like wire.

A sharp intake of breath, then a yelp from W. He swears, gets on his knees and begins whacking the scorching fabric with his crutches.

– Move back! Frau T says. Her voice is very low-pitched, strong, and reverberates in the air like a caged bear, rousing the rest of the compartment. – Back everyone! she repeats.

*Et dimitte nobis debita nostra*, C mutters angrily to himself. Deep down he feels disaster is looming.

They all leap to their feet, close around each other in the corner. L pulls S to her chest. By now, W has reached the carriage door and is trying to open it, yanking at the iron bolt. C hears him strain with effort.

The blaze is starting to take hold, the smoke increasingly thicker, grey and musky. For C and S – for all of them, in fact – the boxcar takes the form of a sealed oven. Flames bloom, vapours rise, and they shield the faces from the embers showering clots of hot ash over their heads in choked panic. It occurs to them they might die like this, though the women are all murmuring reassurances to their crying children, instinctively wrapping them up even more tightly in a space that, in C's opinion, is already far too short of air.

\*

But then, somehow, Frau T jolts the latch from its socket and shouts something, a command or some sort of prayer, and W, tottering on one leg, rams his shoulder against the door and drives it open with all his might.

As they fling the burning mattresses from the train, C watches the tremulous balls of flame until they disappear behind the bend crossed by the long arm of the forest.

And then S leans out and sees, or thinks she sees, the moon rolling out from the clouds, a glob of white in the sky brackish with stars and mist, (it is in fact the one working headlight of a Horch coal truck idling on the crest of a hill, though it's impossible for her to tell from this distance), and then her friends, having shaken the ash from their hair and blown their noses, crowd around the door, and night floods the compartment and they resume breathing normally again, and Frau T's children begin singing a song, *Hänschen Klein*, and the others join in, and S can't help submitting to a flurry of happiness, thinking it must help them for sure, this invincible love of tradition, and music, and while W sinks to the floor, his footless leg, which is singed along the edge of his trouser, resting on top of his good one, his crutches like disarticulated cicada wings beside him, C shuts his eyes and goes on reciting, *Sicut et nos dimittimus debitoribus nostris, et ne nos inducus in tentationem, sed libera nos a malo.* Amen. Amen. Amen.

\*

Frau T crouches down – Are you all right, C?

– Pardon? Yes. His eyes blink open.

– I suppose one gets used to narrow escapes. People do. But we should be there soon.

– Yes.

– And you have big plans?

– Ordinary plans, mostly.

– So that's good. You are young. The war's been over for six years. It's just dragging on a little longer for some of us.

To ensure that she hides her scepticism, eager to give the appearance of confidence, she smiles, except not with her eyes. There are tracings of purple in the hollows beneath them.

When he looks across at his mother, he sees the same thing on her face, only more marked. Her shadowed lids, her colourless lips, her coat tight around her shoulders, her arms wrapped around her chest, the veins tracing her neck, the fuzzed wisps from her greying hair, her strung-out blank expression.

– It can't be much further, Frau T. says. That's what I think.

Sometime in the following dark hours, an old man in the next compartment hangs himself. As the train slows through a station, a woman leaps in, pleads – could the children from the neighbouring cabin she is in to be allowed to join them for the remainder of the journey?

– Of course, says Frau T.

The woman, a wiry seamstress from Tilsit, takes Frau T aside and tells her that the man had been hallucinating periodically throughout the trip, which caused him to weep and scream, and several times someone had tried soothing him by taking him in their arms, but, with his breath shallow and strangled by rage, he'd continued to wail and curse from his broken-toothed mouth: concerned faces hovered over him, but it seemed he saw only the nightmarish guises that belonged to his madness and fear.

Then, at a certain point, he suddenly grew calm. He took stored bits and pieces (a matchbox, a torn-out newspaper article, a coin, a retractable comb, a feather, a bottle top, a small alabaster figurine of a rabbit) from out of the pillowcase he'd converted into a bag. He folded the pillowcase. He put it over his lap and laid everything on top. He closed his eyes, and moaned every so often, but he'd stopped speaking to the air and exploding in bitter rants. When the smoke from the boxcar next door began flooding the carriage, he stood up and moved aside, away from the others: then, while they were distracted, he went to a corner, tied the pillowcase around his neck, strung it from a meat hook and stepped off a steamer trunk.

*

The train kept sliding in the direction of Lübeck across the Schleswig-Holstein lowlands, but S had few ideas of what was meant by their destination.

A little later, in the distance, with the sun behind them, she could make out the needled huddle of spires, like a pincushion, rising from the mound that was the Hanseatic city.

*

The train ground to a halt. There was no station. At first no one understood what was happening, that this was the end of the line. Only when a guard in his grey-green East German uniform stood with his hands on his hips on the tracks in front of the engine did the reality dawn on them: they'd reached No Man's Land.

They filed off the train, shaking themselves like dogs and collecting in one large group, as if awaiting further instructions, the smell of smoke and filth trailing them from the open doors and lingering in the air.

Dotted along the bulldozed strip of forest delineating the border were the patrolling soldiers and through the windows of the watchtowers overhead could be seen the faces of the armed guards studying them.

There were no houses, no shops; the road that was cut out of the slope alongside the forest reminded C of a scar he had on his stomach from where he'd run into an iron girder as a child.

Tethered to a post was a bay horse. You didn't see horses often: at some point after the war, most of them seemed to have disappeared, those that survived the battles and bombing rationed as meat. The horse was big but underfed: C could make out the bones of its ribcage as it tilted its hip to urinate, tendrils of steam emanating from the hot stream in the morning sun, sun felted with tiny spiralling motes in the shafts driven through the trees' branches and in between the shadows of the trunks, as if to spotlight the microscopic habitat or universe of a species newly sprung from the earth.

On the opposite side of the road ran a makeshift-looking barbed wire fence. It flashed against the dark wall of trees like marble flecks in granite. C broke from the crowd and set off across the field in the direction of the woods. He walked steadily through the stubbled grass, with his and his mother's suitcases, praying there were no mines in the area and trusting the others to follow.

The soldiers had gathered at the crest of the road, and stood around gaping with their rifles slung casually over their shoulders. It was plain from the expressions on their faces they had no idea what was going on. The defectors came tramping towards them, but their position didn't waver, and so the refugees kept their eyes down, just went on walking.

L, not surprisingly perhaps, was tempted to stop, re-board the train and head back east again to Güstrow. C turned and ran back to her, shook her lightly, and when she tried to speak and no sound came out he told her in a tone of bristling conviction that in a little less than a day she would be in Lübeck, then Kiel, where her sister-in-law, whom she hadn't seen in over a decade, was living with her children and husband (now that he'd completed his time in prison for war crimes.)

C reminded her that getting away from here, and this – yet another dictatorship – was what mattered most, was all that mattered. And then he said that home was now a place that no longer existed, only in time, in the past, and to prepare for the ways in which they would be transformed by getting out of there.

\*

Over the frozen ground, the refugees pressed on in worried amazement. They passed several guards, avoiding eye contact, advancing in a slow but steady flow towards the border, sometimes calling out an encouragement to one of the children and sometimes taking a hand, or there would be a forced grin, urging each other forward to where they imagined the line to be or a crucial moment determining their new fate. They headed into the forest without stopping. Sometimes, via peripheral vision, they glimpsed one of the troops, standing with his gaze trained on them as they expected, and unwanted images flooded in – Soviet soldiers dragging the coats off smashed blood-spilling bodies, the dangling curl from the inside of a man's skull, a woman with hands unfurled and fingers missing, but they didn't stop walking, avoiding explicit gestures and showing no signs of hesitation, just moving in orderly procession from the sunlight towards the forest's speckled dark.

\*

C's back sagged. There was a log on the track in front. He paused, sat down, resting his feet on his case, and caught his breath, letting the others pass. In the deepest shadows of the woods, he thought he saw the bones of a man, protruding from the undergrowth. But it could have been an animal, a deer perhaps. Or maybe just the broken limb of an elm, twisted into suggestive angles.

Something about the proportions reminded him of his father. At some time as a child, he thought, he'd seen him lie on the grass or forest floor like that, knees up, arms out. He'd been at the lake with his sister and they were drying off after a swim, watching the planes fly overhead through the canopy. He was in a small leafy divot and the sky was clear, so clear he could see the pilot's face as he swooped low over the water, waving, and smell the fuel as the plane jerked sharply and whizzed off.

And then another image came into his mind; a scorched, vivid memory of the soldier who had held them captive in the barn outside Güstrow during Liberation, a Russian infantryman, lying on the grass behind the crooked hedge with the white flowers. Sitting with the soldier, dishevelled and crying, was his mother. The soldier's rifle was resting across his stomach, the tip pointed at her hip, his desire for gold so great, C remembered his mother later saying, that he'd taken the wedding ring from her finger, wrestling so hard in his efforts to get it off he'd almost broken her hand. But C now realised he'd been incredibly naïve and young and stupid. The truth hit him like a blow to the stomach and he tried to put the thought out of his mind, but he couldn't.

*

The section of forest they were passing through was thinner now, the sunlight still cold, but brilliant. From the direction of Lübeck rose fine strands of grey and white smoke, and in Lübeck, they'd been told, the Red Cross took care of displaced persons. They pushed on through the stands of bare elms and poplars and saplings.

– Look, said S, the thistles haven't even lost all their leaves yet.

C heard the whistle of a shrike. When they came though a last cluster of birches, on the far horizon, they saw the city, like a medal on the chest of a dead or sleeping soldier.

S looked at C and laughed and all the children began racing across the fields toward the rising towers and the whole group, possessions bundled in their arms, continued westward, over the cold earth and through the long wheat stalks wet with dew, searching for signs of the nearest road.

– I guess that man in the next carriage didn't believe we'd make it, S said to C, slowing and flinging her bag across her other shoulder.

– No, I guess not, C said.

– His coat was exactly the same colour as the one I wanted for my birthday, she said.

– I didn't see, said C. Come on. It's not as cold as Güstrow, is it?

He was in between her and his mother, who was walking as if through water, without saying a word, almost disembodied, while the surrounding yabberings rose into a steel-blue sky, and for a moment C saw himself as a medieval crusader, a medieval crusader forging his way into some promised land, permanently in exile, but then he heard W, talking as doggedly as ever about his plans, and reality overwhelmed him once more and he resumed the lead.

His mother hurried behind him, stumbling slightly under the weight of her suitcase. In a few hours we'll be in Lübeck, in the West and back with family, thought C. Then he looked with relief at his mother. L's eyes remained fixed ahead, but her cries were as loud as the wind, even though they were trapped inside, and unending. Unending those cries, unending, unending.

# Kabinet of Pink Bits

## Anna
## Hotel Frauenkirche, Dresden 1904

– but how, Diotima thought, can mankind even
have roast chicken without violence?
— Musil

'Do you, dear Berthe, still remember the evening when
Baron von Salmon and Assessor Pike were introduced into
our circle? I'll never forget my horror as I watched them
enter the room and I saw them as two fish.'
— Fanny Lewald

**i**

So here it is again, day opening the night
with its pushy fingers while behind the sounds of the hotel,
steps in the hall, a barking dog, I hear you, breathing
with that rhythmic softness and turning in bed.
I'm not in it: standing at a French door that leads
 onto to a little balcony with a view through a larch tree, my face
is shadowed, a blotched reflection, alone, and pasted
to the glass. By this time tomorrow, you'll be in Prague.

And when you're there? As in the past, the problems
are unremarkable, endless… When I think about the hours,
the dreams we've had together there is a kind of
kitschy refrain that calls, maybe,

maybe, though I have to try and stop the falling tears
while packing my bag with pencils, gloves, two half-filled
manuscript books, one with tunes, one with words,
and a copy of Helene Böhlau's *Halbtier*.

**ii**

I read her a lot when I'm alone. Her writing
holds me more than anyone. Yes,
she is a book I want to read from start
to finish: for I have felt half animal
like her, if writing is, as we say,

art so we won't die of truth. And sometimes
I dream of taking long walks
though I don't know what I'll find;
sometimes I think what I need
is a better form

of camouflage. For there seems to be a thing in me
a thing without courage
that wants to escape
and is ever on the prowl along a path
edged by ditches –

deep ditches or boundary canals
that fill steadily
like cattle troughs, as desire
walks ahead to lead me on
toward the lake:

and hour after hour, day after day
of walking on down roads that part the long grass,
through forest
after forest whose oaks sigh
and are nothing but various greys,

there is a landscape rolling forward
and a fog,
like milk, surrounding
the ravines that sink their teeth into the hills,
toward the lake –

and under which, through patterns
deep-rooted in the earth,
eternal matter twists
and binds all things together –
like words.

**iii**

The hotel's grounds are green and bright but inside the room
there are hollows, clotted with dark.
They disappear across the floor underfoot
and beneath the heavy furniture to the high
rose papered walls.
You and I have put on our clothes silently, though if I listen carefully
the washbasin tap is dripping
that steady light drip that trills
over itself again

and again. I fix my hair at the mirror
and peer
past my shoulder at your face.
You hold my book: a spasm of longing
knocks the sense from my head.
Smooth from swimming the unbroken hours of sleep,
light trickled over your body like roots,
some passage has leapt out
and caught your eye.

> 'A real union, to which
> we had to submit…so quiet and almost solemn, it was therein,
> and we lived in flaccid tubes…'

Your voice continues to work across me
like wind over a pond –

> Crowds on the intercity trains. Dresden
> ham. Not the best place for ham. Frau Grellman
> who thinks she's a physician, settling fever with leeches
> and cigarettes, *'Petr Balek*
> *died. Left me his pocket watch.*
> *Have you ever seen such a nice pocket watch?'*

And the tears begin

### iv

Under that nest of curls I see your pupils expand. Or unfocus.
Seem remote.
Little pools of mind breaking in circles. You're likely to come to it
in time,
you once said to me holding my breast with both hands.
Now you ask
if I will stop waiting. But yesterday I was sitting there
waiting as usual
for everything to separate, watching for the violinist to nod and you
to stand and lower the piano's lid
and leave the stage while the audience clapped and the doors opened,
and I thought, Isn't waiting sometimes a mercy?
And I think now, Aren't you happy enough in the gaps where we live?

But you shrug, say,
> You're twisting the word waiting
> for your own benefit.
> Will you be here when I'm next back from Prague?

*Halbtier*, page one – I offer a line
> '…she agrees she is unconsciously dissatisfied…'

You smile,
> So keep reaching for more.

(Eyelid, your drop of eyelid.)

I spread my arms,
    Yes, maybe that —
    who can say?


**v**

We had spent the afternoon in one of the Zwinger rooms, decked out in
the usual alabaster and silvered brocade.
It's a performance space
I know only too well. I was mildly distracted,
watching a sparrow out the window

while you talked about Hardman Peck uprights
and God.
Resting against the window casement —
watching the bird darting happily, its partner
flapping

underneath the ledge — I was filled by a sudden feeling
of incomprehensible joy,
an unexpected rearrangement
of physical pleasure,
of what must follow,

the law of physics, the fact that stretched between the material and any
small signal
sent to the brain from one or other of the senses
is some sort of ripple; that nothing,
even in death is ever lost.

You got up and came over. You fingered the curve of your jacket,
a habit
you have when the pressure of some irritation with me takes over:
irrepressible offstage and able to talk easily
about one subject and another,

you tend to get edgy when I'm not being attentive,
which gives a tightness
to your wide thin mouth and sometimes exasperates me,
though your voice is lean and supple.
Have you met Walter? you said. But I was preoccupied

and hadn't yet noticed the man, Walter, standing
at your shoulder,
cast in shadow, like a kingfisher at the water's edge.
Then he put out his hand
to take mine, and

that is when I saw him; drawn
in angles of grey wool and silvered-satin trim,
like a silhouette with phosphorescent
edges: I had no idea though, that he would float
all night between my body

and my dreams. And this morning, as I rose from bed ready to write
a few lines, rework a song, the words already seemed
out of context. When I threw my pencils and notebooks into
my little travel bag my hands were trembling,
as if the weight were unbearable.

### vi

The 'woman question' is always there, it seems. Helene Böhlau
went to Constantinople to live outside it.
She was moved by imagination and her love for Friedrich Arndt,
who was married. She moved
to see who she was, for her work, the age-old protection
of the city's towers, hills, domes, defences.
She moved to a new country
out of compulsion
and through creative power,
to test boundaries, avoid insults,
laugh, cry, breathe the sea air.
Sometimes known as Madame Raschid al Bey,

she writes her characters in a way that slides them between disorder
and model citizen.
   *My beloved little owls,* she notes –
   *my own creations, eccentrics, often at odds with the educated aesthetic.*

The girls in her stories get caught out stealing flowers, spying on
neighbours, swinging on gates,
walking backwards through the park,
the dreams bursting out from under their ribs
like spring crocuses through snow.

In Ratsmädel, for example, when Rose grows up she
is looked upon by her father as a commodity in the market,
her betrothed as a magnificent specimen.
That boiled blue carp on the engagement table might be
her body glazed in juices.

And later, when she runs off to the local park,
tossed clear by the wild,
waiting for ghosts,
and stumbles across her betrothed
lying in watch by a lair, hoping to catch the fox –

    'The world is too closed!' he says.

'Yes,' she says, 'that is also why I'm here.'

## vii

Possibly she foreshadows the fate of Isolde in her *Halbtier*, here.
   The way of men and the way of women in households; pale
     young Isolde, grown so weary
with pity for her sister – whose 'beastly' husband
   is endlessly filling her worn out body
       with the godforsaken gift of a twining
umbilical cord –
        that she follows him over the hills,
           shoots him dead in the soft green night.

A longing for the choice to decide who would
			live in her household, and also
		in the house that is herself.

## viii

It reminds me of those mornings when, as a child, my mother
would get my father to fetch the physician
and he would come in,
a tall, camphor-smelling, straight-part-in-his-hair man
in brown suit and polished shoes to give her a little lactophenin
for her nerves. From the doorway –
she needed me there, I think,
for a certain kind of company –
I watched as he snapped the tip of the vial,
drew the mixture into the syringe, pinched a piece of skin on her arm
and injected slowly while she kept
her eyes
closed.
I remember how she'd call me to the side of the bed,
open her eyes and lie
staring at me.
And I remember she would ask in a thin voice,
What was the lesson from all this?
and I didn't know what she hoped I'd say,
something about the need for health perhaps,
the rationing of relief,
the presence of grief, and the experience of pain
on the innermost self. Do not risk going out today, the doctor
would tell her, polishing
the steel curls of the plunger with a piece of chamois cloth,
and I would kiss her flushed cheek.
She took what he said as a
given thing – in relation to herself,
I think she accepted the habits of shutting out

and shutting in. It was some secret buried extension
of who she was that came loose now and then.
The thoughts, drifting up from below,
emerging
and disappearing from the back of where she looked.
My mother continuing to talk weakly about problems,
feeling safe,
everything indefinite,
when only the day before she had supervised the home routines
with such stately, painstaking precision.

Helene knows the Janus-faced vision
of the double burden – the reasons why we continue
to peer through the bars,
why we keep watch through the pieces of light
and give the impression our eyes know
what our bodies are doing;
yet our hopeful pleasure
is often combined
with a sense
of our own helplessness,
(Isolde running in search of justice, redemption, waiting for the sun
to rise, Karl's dead body on the earth, the unattended humbling of her end…)

My mother in linen sheets, shot through
with a little laudanum, smelling of musk,
asking, Are you there?
Yes, Mutti.
Her blank wild smile. Will you read to me?
Yes, Mutti.
The white wings of her
milk hands, her murmuring, The sun's
in your eyes.
Why don't you draw the curtains?

## ix

The foyer is lemony, plush, deserted as we go downstairs, just a couple
of old cats
sitting on the counter washing themselves. Behind the glass doors, the
sounds of maids
as they move furniture to clean. The porter arrives. He loads our bags,
his beard is grey.
He says he knows a short cut to the station; he says, I've never been
outside this city, I've lived here all my days.
He gives you today's newspaper, taps it, nods, smiles, So what do you
think of this man
who wants to build electric locomotives across the country? We see the
picture is of Walter.
Crazy, you say, But who knows what you can do with money.
And there he is,
this man Walter in my mind again, like an unshakeable line
from a song.
Sometimes I think it's the songs that imprison me. You fear
life's basic realities,
you said to me yesterday, I don't envy those dreams. And I said,
How should I cast them off?
You kissed the talk aside. Now shreds of whitish cloud are rising on
the horizon in front of us
as we walk to the station flanked by a warm breeze from the south,
while under the crook
of your elbow you've lodged the folded newspaper

and one of Walter's photographed eyes is fixed on me.
It looks surprisingly docile.
I step nearer to you, the traffic driving plumes of dust across the path.
Your face –
how will I put it? – like a torn dog. Greylag geese flying almost straight
up in the sky,
wings tucked in then paddled out, motion and fragmentation… I can
feel my heart
racing in my chest. Love inserts itself in different ways but over

and over. We die. Everything
is imperfectness. The music that remembers something –

distinguishes something – stays on. It stretches way below the mossy-
green trees,
the five-storey buildings; the old Jewish cemetery in Chemnitz, for example,
where my paternal ancestors
lie with the intimacy of children, no more space than a church choir.
And in between
the tiny spaces, if I go on in this vein for effect, are the boundless words,
songs that are fading
but that still rise in different languages as best they can.


**x**

The first time you left me, back there in Chemnitz,
I had a sensation right through my body
that was like drowning.

The messages in my brain swirled endlessly, whether
I was awake or asleep: thousands of messages.
I tried to shut my ears.

Even the sound of people's feet on the stairs and my mother calling to my
father from the landing made my ears
ring, dissolved in the walls, echoed
through the wallpapered plaster, through the room,
over shelves full of old books and figurines
that seemed to bear witness in their stillness
to the desolate night just endured.
How can such ordinary household noise
make you wonder which side of the world you're on? I said to myself –
Could it be the start of some sort of madness?
which seemed unlikely
though the scraps of thought tied themselves to bits of tunes,
loose bits of tunes that teased me, and hung in my dreams, and wouldn't leave
my head. I came to think of them

as revolutions of longing,
as my hypothetical song cycle.
A personal version of To the Distant Beloved
I suppose. I wanted the songs
to smother separation's voice – to play over the noise of a pain that felt as vast
as the sky – and feeling low in willpower and the impulse toward life,
toward freedom.
I began to think about desire,
and felt sick

and lay in bed
wondering how I could come sometimes feeling guilt
and sometimes happiness; and despair
at the prospect that no one might be able
to fill my being
as you had at the Elisenhof, where we'd made love
in trembling oblivion,
with our minds emptied.

And yet the idea that it was all nothing but desire scared me.

Desire is the pulse of love, I thought,
even a transient,
brief, indecipherable kind of love,
although I had the idea it was
in turning my body towards another

that I was dragged from my own formless, inward reality out
to the social,
from suspicion and from stubbornness, from narrowness
and faint rage
to the realm of other people.

Then after a while, I came to realise
my awful songs were composed of gratitude and a sort
of reined-in aspiration, and I
rode them hard,
gave them names.

*Liebeslied,*
    like the self in a cave seeking light,
        or that swift play of wind through the pines –
      so sentimental, and unquiet,

unquiet with excess of emotion, unquiet
    with the social limits,
      but mostly
unquiet with a failed, wasted longing turned loose, like Rose,
or Effi Briest.

Afternoons, I sometimes wanted to pour my heart down the gutter of
some back alley, get rid of my melodramatic tendencies,
perhaps mould the bit of joy,
the hints of suffering, into some less ridiculous shape. Wishing, too,

  that an accident of birth didn't have to have so much say
  in the future;
  wanting to be both she and he,
  and not be held to some predetermined course.

I saw my mother almost passed out in her room –
she was as beautiful as the moon.
Her questions rising from the bed: she looked
terribly lost, as if she were turning
into emptiness – there with my father or brother-in-law
or the physician… And the question I'd come back to

was the question of why so many men
seemed to act like it was a wisdom on their part
that had made them male.

I had no answers, but the songs kept coming.

*Hinter den Vorhängen*:
    a room filled with comfortable chairs and lavish fabrics,
      and a woman lying in the shape of a fan on her bed, singing
      about the sun-swamped world below her window.

*Lange Nacht*:
> a girl lost in the country, finding her way through the forest by
> moonlight, a moon like a trail of seaweed that slips back
> and forth over the fallen branches in her path.

*Schwan Tränen*:
> set by the cold waters of the ocean, low tide on the Baltic Sea.

*Fliegensong*:
> on the night she almost killed a man in a dream,
> then loved this fact...

And my father, sometimes hearing the singing
coming through the walls of my mother's room, would
beat his breast, laugh. Joke in ways
that would never clear the room
of our loneliness: he said,
a man needs a woman a certain way.
He talked about the dangers of women reading
and of women who couldn't marry,
only curse. And the growing air of disappointment

moved further into the corners of our house
veiled in perfume and cigar smoke,
like the boiler room in our soap factory
with its lye and wood ash,
like that closed-in boiler room
filled with tubs of beef and glycerine.
So at that time, the most entertaining thing for me

was to go down to the piano and sing more songs
play different pieces, get thoroughly worked up
while my father vexed and fumed away in the bedroom above,
a fly in a bloom of fresh dropped cow dung.

Hundreds of hours collapsed onto each other
like this; then in a letter you said, If you want to clear your head
of this pain why not take things at face value?

Why make it so hard? Why not stay one step ahead of your prey?
These thoughts puzzled me.
What am I hunting? I said.

And you explained that this was something we all do,
all the time –
that damage is more or less inevitable.

I just went on wondering.

But at night it was fantastic to lie
and contemplate the black piano
and your black hair; fantastic to read your words

trailing across the pages of your letters,
to imagine
how your hands had brushed the paper
with the same careful workmanship
as on me in my sleep.
In my dreams my tongue came towards you
like an animal.

## xi

Now here on the street, the trams clack along the lines
down to the station.
From a dark, shiny motor car Walter then
steps on to the crowded pavement, effortlessly,
turns towards us, waving
with his leather gloves from Italy in one hand,
surrounded by sun.

## xii

Each day distance works between us, and what we have feels different.
A sonata, the next movement:
the language we now have together
changes like that. A boy in a brown jacket with a dirty collar

plays his flute in the café's doorway.
I listen to its melody,
try holding it in my head.
By the time we've reached the platform it is gone.

### xiii

With his suitcase already in the train,
Walter stands on the step behind and stares.
In the lapel of his jacket is a red geranium.
You smile at him,
but the Dresden Resolution's point, exactly,
manufacturing at such a rate
scares me a little, you say, from under the brim of your felt Homburg,
tipped, as always, slightly to the left.

I feel a swift cooling,
so quick, and dense. Wrapped
in emptiness, I feel I'm at the hilltop
with Isolde on that final dawn.
Your eyes shoot over my head to those of Walter,
Electric trains now, is it?

(Ring of your low voice,
your low voice ringing.)

Our hearts circle the words.
And then we hear the guard's whistle,
and we're turning our bodies into the spring light,
and I hold on as if I were gripping a galloping
horse's neck, I've got to stop myself from falling.

'Life, this is serious…art, that is all just fun,'
    says Helen Böhlau with the steadiness of religion.

### xiv

And here comes your train too,

pulling in.
It is a long morning, and I think we will go,
far from where our days are piled on top of one another.

The glass windows over the station
catch the sun. And another tune comes into my head,

> *Der Flucht Rabe*:
>         a raven on a minaret, satin throat, coalish eye,
> scanning the wind – even from a distance
> love recognises what it can't name.

# Epic Angels

## Celia
## Sydney, 2011

I wish I were a glow worm
a glow worm's never glum
Cause how can you be grumpy,
when the sun shines out your bum?
— unknown

**Saying It – Saying What??!!**
**Blog Instalment Number 2. Woo Hoo!!**

Don't know if anyone is actually reading this post, but if so, thanks... Yer, so have managed to survive one whole week at college now. pros: super great people, amazingly clever and talented, mostly adorable and fun, and the bar: cons: some people make really bad music choices and EARLY MORNING classes!! Anyway trying to get some life admin done and end up doing this. Avoidance technique. Ummm just looking to overhaul my brain like pretty much everyone. For example after trying to work out a practice question for 'government' for days I finally realised I meant to write 'is the basis for of capitalism,' not 'cannibalism.' True story. Haha.

Is anyone else doing that thang of watching Buffy and Community and Sherlock and Boosh and Ryan Gosling in anything he's in to calm the nerves? It's heaps fun watching Harry Potter and trying to read it at the same time. It is possibly the greatest challenge of my life.

About
Archive: 2011 (1)
Edit
Work and education
Relationship: Horatio Farmer
Friends: 737
Family: Yer
Quotes: I don't really live by a quote, wish I did?
Places Lived

> Edit
> Sydney, Australia
> Current location

> Edit
> Braidwood, New South Wales
> Home town

> Edit
> Brunswick, Victoria
> Moved here

> Edit
> Kangaroo Valley, New South Wales
> Moved here

> Edit
> Jindabyne, New South Wales
> Parents have moved here

And I love Dr Who as all you who know me out there know and I know that 'Blink' is thought of as Dr Who lite, but I was in Jindabyne last weekend and watched it again as a way of trying to introduce my mum to one of my favourite shows. (Anything not to have to walk up the hill and sit looking at the lake like she does EVERY DAY and tries making me do when I'm there too.) She actually managed to appreciate that the Doctor has something to offer. For me, it's things like Dr Who and Harry Potter that are home. There are books and shows that live inside me. They are part of me. I'll be feeling one thing and after them I'll be feeling completely different. They seem to call to me. They'll pop into my mind sometimes, even when they're not something I'm thinking about at all.

tbh it's possibly a warped version of homesickness. While I was thinking about the quantum locked angels and how Sally Sparrow's not allowed to blink, I felt annoyed again that I didn't have a sister or brother and wanted someone proper to talk to. The truth is that I couldn't help thinking it would possibly be good to have someone on my side for once, just like having been made to move round all the time has possibly been the freaking hardest aspect to my life, and like with the frozen angel statues (haha) everything happens when no one's looking and possibly everyone's ruled by their desire to be seen, and that happiness is sudden and fast and indescribable and possibly the most needed emotion in the world, because it's so easy to forget it right away. Anyway, having already seen the episode loads, I could watch and use my i-pod at the same time so listened to the Foals for the hundredth time. No such thing as too much!! I say fun and music make up the world.

question 1. on formspring yesterday: If you had to give up one thing you do daily for a year, what would it be?'
Being sad? Nah – it's all sunshine and bubbles!!

My grandmother came for an afternoon too which was cool. She is nice, even though I'd forgotten how scary she is. It's the way she looks at you, her foregn accent etc.

*Dad told me he was proud of me…*
*It was for picking up and passing him the remote with my feet…*

*'What does a bluetooth look like?' – my mum*

What else? As a way to start getting myself
ready for comic-con I'm dying my hair red…

Not sure why I'm writing any of this.
Dumping stuff is a new phenomenan for me. (and my spelling is crappy as ever, sooorry)

The contradictions. Yer, the contradictions… "Life goes on." (Though sometimes it doesn't!)

Anyway, HERE I AM AT UNI AND ON FACEBOOK –
WHOO TECHNOLOGY!!!
I LIKE PINEAPPLE KISSES SO COME AT ME BEHBEH!!

## Blog has been removed

Sorry, the blog at in-the-sky.blogspot.com has been removed. This address is not available for new blogs.

# October in the Northern Hemisphere

## M and her Mother
## Poland, 2014

> Tell all the truth but tell it slant
> – Emily Dickinson

M and her mother had flown to Europe. In three weeks of holidaying they would visit family in Hamburg, Celle, Ratzeburg, Berlin, then cross the border into Poland to see the place where M's mother grew up: a kind of uncovering, genealogical reckoning. M had made a few journal entries at her cousins', and some more now on the train to Walcz, but she had never been to this part of Europe before and mostly she devoted her time to taking in the landscape.

At first, gazing out the compartment window, the forests and mountains seemed familiar, as if the trees and the *Hochsitze*, those little wooden hunting towers, blurrily flashing past were the backdrops to movies. Gradually, though, what she was looking at began to feel strange. M had flown to Germany with her mother because her mother had collected enough frequent flyer points for a free flight, and after the fall of the Iron Curtain she'd wanted to see her hometown again. M, after avoiding this part of the world all her life, now wanted to see it too. Neither of them spoke much in the train, as if they were commuters on their way home from work although, at one point, M's mother leant across to show M a passage in a book she'd had open on the same page for the past hour, a memoir by a Melbourne writer, Vincent Buckley, which made mention of M's father, briefly and schematically. M nodded, told her mother she'd seen it before, then, replacing her sunglasses, turned back towards the scenery.

In Walcz, they waited at the station to meet up with M's mother's cousins, B and her brother Z, who like M's mother were in their early seventies, and who were joining them for the week. The train was late, so M and her mother spent forty-five minutes standing on the platform, where traces of the old Deutsch-Krone sign were still visible under the paint. For a moment, M thought about calling her husband and daughter back home, but calculating the time difference she worked out that in Sydney it was 3 a.m. Finally the train on which Z and B were travelling arrived, and they all kissed, and took a taxi to the Bialy Domek, checked in and went up to their rooms, washed, changed, then went downstairs to have supper in the dining room.

The next morning it was raining. M got up before her mother was awake, showered, put on warm clothes and went out for a walk. The hotel was on a street corner that was nowhere near the centre of town, so M decided to simply go round the block because she didn't want to get lost, and she couldn't speak any Polish. The block seemed the biggest she'd ever walked. There were long stretches of concrete and mesh fencing, behind which were building sites with motionless cranes and bulldozers, big holes in the earth, half-built walls, brick bases, pillars and little roped-off trees.

When she'd made a circuit, returned to the hotel and met the others in the dining room for breakfast, B asked M's mother if she knew that this was the place where both their parents had held their wedding receptions.

No I didn't, said M's mother.

M looked at Z and B. They were both broad-faced, big-boned, with the same pale-coloured eyes and shaped faces as her mother. It wasn't easy for them to hold an involved conversation in English so they switched to German, but M had trouble following, and so taking out a book she began to read.

The dining room was dark and they were the only people there: M moved her chair closer to the light, resting her coffee on the adjoining table. The book, picked up from a stand at the front of a second-hand store in Friedrichshain and which she had been reading for the past two days, was a collection of short stories by Katherine Mansfield, called *In a German Pension*. In her twenties, M had read a couple of stories and though she'd liked them, it was only now, in these Pension stories, that she was struck by the surprising bravery of the writing. How old had Mansfield been when she died? Thirty-two? Thirty-four? A precocious, if sometimes vicious, bisexual woman, wary about human relationships, yet at the same time unafraid to cut them wide open and draw out all their entrails. At twenty-two, sent by her mother after a miscarriage to a clinic in Bavaria, she'd written these pieces in an atmosphere of stuffiness and hypocrisy. M could easily picture the surroundings. And the figure of Mansfield appeared from the shadows like a kind of mirage in the room, standing there with her own mother at her back, cutting the light, her silhouette grown large with assertions and reproach, and then M closed her eyes for a moment and they were gone.

When they'd finished breakfast, M and her relations put on their coats and began exploring the suburbs of Walcz. The rain had stopped, but M could still feel the cold working its way through the wool of her jacket. B, a neat, compact woman with round cheeks and sporting dazzling white hair cut in the shape of a helmet, led them to the city centre, a bland square intersected by geometrical garden beds, built around a fountain that didn't run, then brusquely directed them along the street to the Lutheran church.

Gradually, over the following days, M would come to realise that the hint of impatience in B was a strategy to conceal the destabilising effects of walking through a place she identified as her homeland and which was now another country; but at the time M put it down to German passion for method and organisation, or efficiency.

You know St Anthony castrated himself? said Z to the three women.

They shook their heads. They were standing by a statue of the saint outside the church. Leaves scattered along the footpath from the trees overhead. B gave a snort, then waved them on again without saying a word and took off down the road. M's first thought was that they were going to look at the rear of the old church, where she imagined there might be a cemetery, but B went past the church's high iron fence and disappeared round the corner. They compliantly followed.

Helped by the map she'd kept from a trip two years earlier, B then proceeded to take them to further points of interest from childhood: the primary and secondary schools, the sports field where the Hitler Youth and League of German Girls staged their sports and entertainment activities, the house on the main street that had been the office of the family business as well as home. The house was surprisingly substantial, four-storeys high, and painted pink in contrast to the grey it had been in the pre-war years. They took photos of each other smiling in front and went back to the hotel.

In the room she was sharing with her mother, M lay on the bed with her book while her mother went down to the bar to get a gin and tonic. As she looked at her mother's dressing gown hung carefully on the back of the door, M felt the rising tension of an animosity she'd thought long left behind, an oversized child, as it were, and opened her book. That morning she'd left off midway through Mansfield's *The Swing of the Pendulum*, and although she'd noticed the tone of snootiness towards the Germans in it like the others (Was that why she'd leapt on these stories? she wondered), as she read, M tried to pay attention to the ways in which the writing stirred a kind of loyalty for its main character, Viola – penniless, cooped up in a pension, contemplating the consequences of the decisions she's about to make on the rest of her life – and how the words built up an air of menace, subtle but distinctive. M sensed a terrible fragility in the story. She liked the ambivalent sentiments in the writing. The phrase about Viola's room, 'full of sweet light and the scent of hyacinth flowers', brought to mind spring in Melbourne when she was nine and her father had taken her with him on a house call – a kindly old couple in Malvern where they'd fed her cake while she waited in their sitting room. They'd owned a chain of department stores.

Whatever happened to the Steinbergs? M asked her mother, who opening the door was entering the room with a near empty glass.

Her mother looked confused. The Steinbergs? she said.

Those patients of Dad's in Malvern, M said, with the beautiful garden.

Oh, they died, said her mother, shrugging. They had wonderful taste, she said, and setting her drink on a side table and going into the bathroom to tidy her hair, she called out to M, suggesting they go together to the bar again before dinner.

She always spoke in a manner that was very assured, but often also affectionate, reflected M. So she put on her shoes, dug out a jumper, and when she came out again her mother was waiting in the corridor.

That night, the dining room was busy. M would have preferred to try somewhere different in town, but she was there in part due to the generosity of these people and at the very least should appear agreeable and friendly, she knew that. B and Z had chosen a table and were sitting talking quietly, each with a bread roll and a beer in front of them. Z stood to pull out the chairs for M and her mother. They sat and began discussing the places they'd seen that day and M joined in the conversation, for some reason feeling as if she were a particularly incompetent actor in a play or film and what was happening had nothing to do with reality.

B told Z to be sure of what he planned to order when the waiter approached.

Yes, yes, said Z, a bearish man with a silver beard like Ian McKellen. He was a retired agriculturalist and seemed lonely. He attempted to cut his roll. It's so hard you could ride it, he said, in a cheerful voice.

They all laughed.

Throughout dinner, they stuck to talking about their everyday lives. M asked Z what he had done as a forester. It wasn't something she'd heard of outside fairy tales.

Z ran through the high points of his career; a degree in environmental science, conservation work in the central German woods, a job in the Philippines helping in the fair trade sales of banana chips, improved cattle programs. A breed of cattle for the developing world, he said, which eats less and provides more meat.

Oh for God's sake, said B, rolling her eyes, don't start on about your cows.

Earlier, at the rear of the old family home, Z had pointed out the concrete slab of what had been a chicken shed when they were children. Where they'd housed the Russian prisoners of war working for us, he said. Z spoke about things in a way that seemed to embarrass the two older women. He told them that the prisoners had been used in the parents' factories from 1941. They were kept there till the end of 1944. His mother, he said, reminding him of their own need for food by the end, had ticked him off for giving the prisoners bread. But he continued to do it, he said, because they were working and hungry, you know? and he'd fed a pet cat of one of the prisoners as promised, when the group were moved on to a camp in a neighbouring town.

Z had a vast, vast knowledge of Nordic mythology, but he forgot to check for traffic when crossing the road and didn't know how to get money from an automatic teller machine. How much, wondered M, did he recall things the women couldn't seem to remember, and how much did the women simply not want to learn about their earlier lives? The more M asked Z and B about their parents, their jobs, their life in postwar Germany, the more she sensed a growing unease. B shooshed her brother impatiently and got M to tell them about her daughter, her husband, what it was like living in Australia.

Over the next three days, the four of them wandered together through the streets of Walcz: cold, a fine, constant drizzle, lanes of grey cobbled stone lanes of grey damaged concrete. They located the childhood homes of extended family, occasionally stopping at buildings that struck some nostalgic chord. Sometimes B and Z and M's mother would amuse themselves remembering something from the past. They watched swans buffet the little waves of the lake behind the yacht club boathouse, and peered over the hedge at the house where Eva Braun once stayed, which stood in the middle of a shambolic yet beautiful garden. Each night they ate in the hotel dining room and talked things over in stilted bouts of conversation, and when the others had gone to their rooms, M and her mother would linger, drinking the last of the wine and chatting to the Polish waiters and waitresses.

On their fourth night there, as their plates were being cleared, M's mother threw her hands on her chest all of a sudden and, What about we go to the lake tomorrow, she asked, where my father used to take me as a child?

M looked at her mother. She was strong-boned, still handsome, with salt and pepper coloured hair gathered and swept into a crown-shaped bun on her head. Her eyes were pale blue and she wore no make-up except for a touch of lipstick. From the expression on her face, it seemed there was something she was attempting to fathom, a flash of something recognised and then lost. Apparently her father had saved her from drowning in the one of the local lakes when she was two or three. M imagined her mother as a little girl, running through the big house they'd visited earlier, when her family had been well-off and everything had had a different name (they'd lived on the main street, for example, called Adolf Hitler Strasse, like many streets in Germany at the time), unaware of just how much everything was about to change.

But the following day B wanted to walk to one of the other lakes closer to town. She made a time for them to meet after breakfast. Have you got an umbrella? she asked M.

I don't want to carry it, M said. A waterproof jacket is fine.

While she was getting her phone and putting on her jacket, M's mother asked her if she remembered seeing the framed photo above the piano in her house of her as a baby on a balcony in her mother's arms. M nodded.

I wish I could see it again, her mother said.

What do you mean? said M.

I wish we could go inside, look around, her mother said. She was pinning a gold brooch to her scarf and gazing out the window.

The trees were turning. The leaves rattled on the branches, like ghosts. Beyond the grounds' walls, as the cranes and construction work started up, rain spattered across the roofs of the row of adjoining houses.

I wish I could ring the bell and they'd let me stand on that balcony, but it's now a restricted building.

A government building? asked M. She noticed a stray strand of hair hanging down her mother's back, lifted it and wound it round the bun, tucking it into a hairpin.

Yes, said her mother, It was seized by the communists as soon as they marched in and remained their headquarters until they left.

In town it was market day. They strolled through the covered stalls selling vegetables, T-shirts, shoes, outdated CDs. For her mother and perhaps to please B, M bought a small folding umbrella. The stallholder, wearing an oversized mac, with dyed blonde hair, pointed at a rack of clear plastic ponchos and told them when walking in this kind of weather she put on one of these, but then she looked at them and shook her head, and laughed, and M and her mother laughed too, only they were not quite sure what they were laughing about.

When they reached the lake, Z and B struck off along the path, in single file with their umbrellas held aloft, ahead of M's mother (who limped slightly due to a bad hip and forced M to lag) and talking between themselves, and for a moment M felt a rush of melancholy, something to do with the strangeness of her mother, the childlike passiveness in her every move, which stopped M's irritation hardening into rage.

As her cousins continued without stopping, M's mother talked about her husband (M's father), who'd been dead for years; then gestured towards a cemetery where her paternal grandfather was supposedly buried. M didn't understand why no one else was interested in going in until later the next day in the museum. There, she learned that, taken as part of the first partition by the Prussians from the Polish in 1772, Walcz was returned to Polish administration in 1945, all Germans were expelled and everything relating to them destroyed.

At the end of the path there was a café. At first M thought she was in a state of mind where she'd be better off spending some time alone. But Z was expecting them to eat together, especially since there had finally been a break in the weather, and before she'd a chance to extricate herself B shouted them a round of beers.

Just as they were sitting down, a text came in from M's husband, long and somewhat cryptic, mainly about their daughter, but there were also some reports about the music he was writing for a feature film.

M frowned at her phone. For a while, she tapped at the screen, composing a reply, hearing the fricative exchange of the others speaking beside her, until she realised, despite not really knowing the language, sitting at a table with her relations involved socialising, and put her phone away without sending off anything.

After lunch, M disappeared to the bathroom, rinsed her mouth, buttoned up her black coat, and went out to the others again. Unlike her cousins, M's mother didn't want to return to the hotel to rest. She suggested they take a cab on their own to Lake Raduń. All her memories of her father seemed to centre on that one dreamlike memory where he'd jumped into the water and paddled out to save her, though in that memory her father is someone she perhaps realised she had barely known in real life: blurred by water whose sinuous currents seemed to be passing right through him: he was, she said, wreathed in the silver blue tendrils of the lake, haloed or godlike. She told M that sometimes when she had dreams about him he laid his hand on her shoulder, she could feel the weight of it, and for a moment on waking she thought he was right there in front her. Once, she said, she woke up and thought she could smell his cigar smoke in the room.

How old were you when you last saw him? asked M, who only knew him from a couple of faded photos.

I was seven when he was captured by the Russians and made a prisoner of war, said her mother, very young.

At the lake they gazed out across the water. Insects. Silty reeds. A suspension bridge. Black woods to the shore. In keeping with a visit stamped by memory, M bought her mother an ice cream: the building, her mother said, was virtually unaltered. For a while, she talked about the years before she, her brother and their mother, Leni, had had to evacuate. Those were the only happy days of my mother's life, she said, But then we had to leave with nothing but what we could carry, and then a few years later we had to flee again, this time from the East to the West. She talked about her uncle, Fritz, her mother's twin brother, how they'd been separated as babies – illegitimate, their mother couldn't afford to keep both, and Leni had spent her childhood in orphanages and foster homes. Reunited as teenagers, they'd become close, some thought too close, M's mother said, although she doubted there was any truth to this. At twenty-seven, in order to appear legitimate so that she could marry, Leni's one maternal aunt, Klara, had officially adopted her. Then, in the years following the war, Leni struggled to make enough to support her own children, since her husband never returned from the gulag, so she took jobs, in potato fields or factories, whatever she could find, in spite of being in her late forties by this stage, and not physically strong. And although she'd remained in touch with her birth mother, M's mother had met her grandmother only once, introduced to her as 'Aunt Anna'.

You can see, M's mother said, why I couldn't ever tell your father any of this. It would have upset him, and he didn't need to know.

M hid her face. This kind of middle-class conservatism was hard to understand, if not completely crazy. M then asked her mother about what was now known to have been going on all around them throughout those years: prisoners deported in trains through the military town and transferred to camps, west to Belzec, Chelmno, Treblinka, south to Auschwitz-Birkenau.

Her mother shrugged. The only thing we could think about was survival, she said. We just had to move forward.

M reflected on her mother's words. Forward, forward, forward. And the impression she had was that those words refused all challenge.

So they walked in silence along the path to the jetty. The jetty was long and newly restored: it was constructed from wide pale boards secured with massive bolts, and jutted out into the water that mirrored an image of it back to them, enhanced by the muted shapes of the reflected trees. The surface of the lake was brown except for a patch of wavering blue in the distance where the clouds had opened to reveal a section of sky, and there was a line of rowboats upturned on the shore opposite that appeared not to have had the sludge cleaned off them in years.

M's mother took a few steps along the jetty and peered into the shallows, which swayed with underwater grasses like tongues. After a moment, she draped her arm over M's shoulder, tapped the toe of a shoe on the jetty's edge; her skin smelt faintly soapy.

M asked if this was the place where she'd fallen in and her father had rescued her.

Her mother said, Yes, and gestured to a spot, adding this was where they would sit in summer when they picnicked here.

Till when? asked M.

Till we had to evacuate, of course, said her mother.

And this was an Olympic training facility? asked M.

Yes, but it was open to the public too, said her mother.

For a while, they stood together, gazing at the cool leaden pool of the lake.

It's beautiful, said M's mother.

M thought so too.

Her mother then began to talk about her time at Güstrow in the Eastern bloc, which M hadn't realised was where she'd first moved to with her family from here, and the most interesting part was the glimpse she had of her mother's adolescence in another massive familial home, across the road from the city's spectacular rose garden, a four-storey house where month by month it was ordered that they take in more and more refugees until they were reduced to living in the one room. M saw her mother's eyes bright and gleaming, but her face in the shadows looked calmly impassive, a way of holding herself M recalled from the past whenever they'd struggled over something.

Let's walk via the woods, her mother said, and they set off along what appeared to be the main trail through the forest.

A little time later, after taking lakeside paths all the way back to town, as they were walking down the main street back to the original residence, M tried to remember a line from a Katherine Mansfield story she'd read the day before, something about ignorance. Something about the mystery of birth and the simplicity of death.

Her mother asked if there was anything on her mind. But M felt too muddled to muster the right tone for these sorts of subject and said, No, not really, smiling in a way that she hoped would do.

Mansfield never told her husband John Murry the story of her baby, thought M. Then, glancing at her mother, thought, Her father, her mother, her brother, no one left.

On the way, M's mother stopped to peruse clothes shops and bought a piece of plum cake. I deserve it, she said, and M couldn't tell whether she was joking or not.

They got to the house.

Will we knock? asked M.

Her mother looked askance, said they couldn't do that.

In fact, the door was open. A couple of painters in overalls came out carrying a ladder. They wore baseball hats pushed down on their foreheads and looked good-natured.

Without saying anything, M went into the entrance hall, climbed the stairs draped in drop sheets. She glanced round, saw her mother following, an expression of mild alarm on her face.

When they reached the landing on the first floor, tense and slightly breathless, M's mother gripped the balustrade and gazed down the corridor.

This was our floor, she whispered, our parlour, all of our bedrooms. Certain things were the same; she indicated the ceiling, some of the light fittings, but the rooms had been divided and converted into multiple offices. The door to the room in front was ajar. My mother's sitting room, she said, and even before she said another word M sensed this was the room with the balcony in the photograph of her mother and grandmother from so long ago.

Leaning through the doorway, M saw it was empty and pulled her mother in. Her mother crossed to the window, the heels of her flat leather shoes making no sound on the covered boards.

The French doors to the balcony were locked, but M's mother made a frame around her face with her hands and pressed it against the glass. It looks just as it did, her mother said, except there are no window boxes filled with red geraniums.

She's going to cry, thought M, and went over to her.

When her mother turned, however, she was smiling, her cheeks flushed. Her hands were cupped around her face. I can't believe it, she whispered, I never thought I'd see this again.

The dead are always walking in front of us, thought M. And she knew she should make some kind of move toward her mother, do something like hug her, but she didn't, couldn't. Later on, she would recall this moment with a baffled sweep of sadness and estrangement, one that flashed its way into her head over and again like the tail of an eel.

They went downstairs; M's mother wanted to go around to the back to see if the cellar still existed, and she talked about her experiences during wartime, the routine and fear of the nightly air raids. The entrance to the cellar was bricked up, and, having retraced as much as she could, they returned to the hotel.

Z and B were surprised to hear that they'd managed to get inside the old home, but when M's mother began to tell them about the state of things, it was clear they were not really interested.

The next day, they were taking the train back to Berlin. They rose early, at six. M hoped to make a final walk before breakfast around the town, along the main street and past the old barracks, now transformed into flats.

Her mother had finished showering and stood in front of the mirror in order to put up her hair. It hung in a braided rope down her back. She wore a muslin shawl over her shoulders to protect her clothes. Her skin was glistening. And her hip was giving her less trouble. It was the painkillers her doctor had provided, which she only used every so often. She pinned and clasped her bun, and while M was showering called to her through the door. You know their father, she said, meaning Z and B, He was the only one who was an actual Nazi.

This gave M a chill, but for some reason she laughed.

No really, said M's mother. He spent three years in jail after the war.

M got out of the shower, wrapped a towel around her. What did he do?

I don't know, said her mother. He was an accountant. I think he was involved in some sort of government affairs in Berlin.

When M came out of the bathroom, her mother sat with her handbag in her lap, organising her passport and tickets.

Is it true, what Z said yesterday, asked M as she dried herself, that he thought my father was such a suspicious-sounding character he hired a private detective to have him checked out?

But her mother ignored the question, or pretended she hadn't heard.

M dressed in her jeans and walking shoes and glanced at her mother sitting on the bed in front of her in her cream blouse and pearl earrings. She seemed very calm.

So dear, she said to M, ready and packed? Then, looking over and seeing M had put on her coat and scarf, asked, Where are you going?

M could hear the chiding note in her voice.

This is the last breakfast together, her mother said, and shut her bag and clasped her hands over it.

As if on cue there was a knock on the door.

Clearly determined to avoid what could descend into an argument, Coming, said M's mother.

B called out to them from the corridor, they were on their way to the dining room, would they all go together?

There was an expression of grim wilfulness on M's mother's face. M didn't quite know how to respond. She felt sick. For a moment, her conscience wrestling with what she wanted, she tried to collect herself. She swallowed hard. Then she picked up her phone, her book, her bag, and after fighting off the desire to cry, or flee, she went and opened the door and followed her three older relations downstairs.

Two hours later, as they left Walcz, its misted bodies of water gliding into the dark woods, M was relieved. While they'd been there, she had felt an involuntary rise of shame and panic in herself, and towards Germany. In the train's bathroom, she caught sight of her face in the mirror; it had a hard or cynical appearance she thought, or perhaps it was just stolid. There were rings under her eyes.

She called her husband and daughter and spoke as naturally as she could, but she could tell she sounded like she was on another planet: from the way they were talking with their voices slightly flat, she realised they must have been watching TV or getting ready for bed.

So, how is it going? asked her husband.

Fine, M said. How is it there?

Okay. No, good, we're managing, he said. Has it been interesting travelling with your mother? he asked.

It has, M said. And she thought about Katherine Mansfield getting through her various kinds of exile. And she thought about her mother and the questions that, in spite of everything, just couldn't be asked, or would never be answered.

Later, back home in Sydney, in the course of retelling people moments from the journey, she'd laugh, and talk about the awful side of things, the small skirmishes day after day, the heart-wrenching rigid force of differences.

But for now, seated again next to her mother, who was still holding the Vincent Buckley book, a gold pendant on her throat glinting in the sunlight, the wide open world rushing past the window, M leant across, took her mother's hand in hers, felt the joy of movement and the pleasure of watching two birds blaze a trail across a blue, blue sky. And then the panic returned.

# Notes

References are made to the following authors and works:

Epigraph: Eva Hoffman, *After Such Knowledge* (Public Affairs NY, 2004)

Arrival: Georg Trakl, *En route*

Fragmentblatt (Leaf Fragments): Robert Walser, *Oppressive Light: Selected Poems by Robert Walser* (trans. Daniele Pantano, Black Lawrence Press, 2012)

    Johann Wolfgang von Goethe, The Sorrows of Young Werther

In the Wind's Way: Virgil, *Aeneid*, Book II (trans. Robert Fitzgerald, Penguin, 1985)

Wasserturm (Water Tower): Federico Garcia Lorca, *Ballad of the Spanish Civil Guard* (edited by F.G. Lorca and Donald M. Allen, 1961)

Dear Sister: Hölderlin, *The Rhine: Hymns* (trans. Michael Hamburger, Penguin, 1998)

The Masurian Lakes: Alfred Döblin, *Berlin Alexanderplatz* (trans. Eugene Jolas, Continuum, 2004)

Second Language: Patrick White, *Voss* (Readers Union, 1959)

    Paul Bowles, *The Sheltering Sky* (John Lehmann, 1949)

What Name Will You See When You Do Not Hear a Sound?: Cervantes, *Don Quixote* (trans. Peter Motteux, Everyman, 1975)

Rope in the Snow: Arthur Rimbaud, *Childhood: Enfance II* (trans. Oliver Bernard, Penguin, 1954)

Kabinet of Pink Bits: Robert Musil, *The Man Without Qualities* (trans. Sophie Wilkins, Knopf, 1995)

    Fanny Lewald, *A Modern Fairy Tale (1854): The Queen's Mirror* (trans. Shawn C. Jarvis and Jeannine Blackwell, University of Nebraska Press, 2001)

    Helene Böhlau, *Halbtier* (Fleischel, 1903)

    Beethoven, To the Distant Beloved (Op. 98, 1816)

    Theodor Fontane, *Effi Briest* (1896)

October in the Northern Hemisphere: Emily Dickinson, *Tell all the Truth but Tell it Slant: The Poems of Emily Dickinson* (Harvard University Press, 1998)

    Katherine Mansfield, *In a German Pension* (Hesperus, 2005)

www.ingramcontent.com/pod-product-compliance
Lightning Source LLC
Chambersburg PA
CBHW070907080526
44589CB00013B/1207